Faith Founded on Fact

Essays in Evidential Apologetics

by
JOHN WARWICK MONTGOMERY

THOMAS NELSON INC., PUBLISHERS
NASHVILLE   NEW YORK

Fourth printing

Copyright © 1978 by Thomas Nelson Inc

Library of Congress Cataloging in Publication Data

Montgomery, John Warwick.
  Faith founded on fact.

  Includes bibliographical references and indices.
  1. Apologetics—20th century—Addresses, essays, lectures. I. Title.
BT1102.M65   239′.0904   77-28048
ISBN 0-8407-5641-0

For
JEAN A. COLLIER
A contemporary Maecenas

Contents

Preface

No one—the old adage has it—wants to buy a pig in a poke. Much less will the serious reader want to cope with a theological argument hidden under a bushel. What, then, is "evidential apologetics" and why should a book of essays on that subject be worth perusing?

The term "apologetics" once designated one of the three main branches of systematic theology, the others being dogmatics and ethics. Dogmatics set forth in organized, topical form the doctrinal content of Christian belief; ethics did the same for the practical, moral consequences of Christian dogma. Apologetics offered a *defense* (Gr. *apologia*) for the doctrinal and ethical content of biblical religion.

Today, however, there is not a theological seminary in the world (to my knowledge) that gives the same stress to apologetics as it does to dogmatics or ethics—unless one thinks of certain liberal schools of theology where the three fields are equalized by placing no significant stress on any of them. The lack of emphasis on the defense of Christian faith in our time is especially unfortunate—and ironic—when one reflects that ours is a time of secularism demanding that Christians "be ready always to give an answer [Gr. *apologia*] to every man that asks you a reason of the hope that is in you" (1 Pet. 3:15). This is perhaps more true than in any other period in history since the apostolic age. The present book of essays endeavors—without "apology" (the weakened modern sense of the word)—to offer just such answers.

But why speak of *"evidential* apologetics"? Is not such an expression redundant—indeed pleonastic? How could there be a defense of Christianity without the marshaling of evidence in its behalf?

In the most profound sense, a "non-evidential" apologetic *is* a contradiction in terms, roughly equivalent logically to a "square circle." The Greek word *apologia* was employed classicly as a technical term in the law. It referred to that case which the defendant presented on the basis of testimonial and material evidence. A defense, then as now, depended squarely on the factual evidence marshaled—no evidence, no defense. In the history of the law, this point was handsomely expressed by Lord Mansfield in 1746, when as solicitor general he argued in the proceedings against Lord Lovat for treason (18 Howell State Trials, 812): "There is no calling witnesses without facts; there is no making a defence without innocence; there is no answering evidence which is true."

Yet, as essays in the present work amply show, influential attempts are being made to create systems of apologetics that supposedly do not depend on factual evidence but instead rely upon "assertively true" presuppositions or "faith-informed" starting points. Such positions are either unabashedly "presuppositionalist" (arguing that the Christian has every right to start from his unprovable first principles, for the non-Christian is doing the same thing from *his* philosophical point of departure) or more subtly metaphysical (stating that the Christian's worldview, though it cannot be proven by any particular evidential considerations or by any specific, concrete facts, nonetheless in some sense explains the universe more "comprehensively" or "coherently" than do all alternative views). It is difficult to find in the latter approach anything significantly different from what is presented by the former. Neither allows evidence to arbitrate ultimate questions of religious truth. Christianity does indeed offer the most comprehensive solution to the human dilemma, but apart from the marshaling of brute fact to prove this, the claim is worth no more than that of any other religion or philosophy leading to maximal comprehensiveness or coherence. And if only Christians are in a position to identify what is truly "comprehensive," "coherent," or "ultimately true," then apologetics is an exercise in perfectly circular reasoning, that is, in perfect futility.

This author rejects all such presuppositionalisms. The flight from "verification" shared both by theological liberals, (whose theologies *ought* to fear testability) and by metaphysically inclined evangelicals (whose theologies deserve far better at their hands) is a retreat from the apologetic task laid upon all Christians by the apostolic witness itself. The fact that A. J. Ayer and other contemporary logical positivists defined "evidence" too narrowly in developing the principle of verification in no way vitiates the principle itself. In its simplest form the principle merely states that if factual assertions are to be sensible, they must at least be subject to evidential testability, for that which is compatible with anything and everything says nothing. To deny this is to open the floodgates to metaphysical nonsense (of which the history of philosophy and the history of religions have offered illustrations *ad nauseam*) and to remove Christianity's most powerful cognitive weapon in a pluralistic world—the factually attestable sword of the Spirit, the Word of God.

This book begins with an introductory essay dealing critically with the most influential recent effort to substitute a theological metaphysic for evidential apologetics: Carl F.H. Henry's *God, Revelation and Authority*. The problems in Henry's approach lead naturally to a search for a better way. We therefore find ourselves considering, first, what place reason should have in the proclamation and defense of Christian faith. Is reason an enemy or a friend and how can it be made to serve its proper function? (chapter one).

The case for Christ's resurrection from the dead has always been the fundamental evidential apologetic for Christianity. Hence, in chapter two, we concentrate on the philosophical soundness of the argument for the miracle in light of the most recent literature on the subject. In chapter three, we examine the need to engage in an active apologetic for the Easter miracle. The focus of chapter four is the superiority of Christian argument over that of other religions (such as the oft-equated "historical religion" of Islam) owing to Christianity's ability to vindicate Christ's deity by the historical evidence for His resurrection. Chapter five presents Dr. Samuel Johnson as a most winning illustration of the many Christian thinkers who have treated the historical resurrection miracle as the fundament of their own case for the truth of the faith. For those still weighing the possible merits of presuppositional apriorism, a literary-philosophical analysis of the contemporary apologetic viewpoint of Cornelius Van Til, as set forth in chapter six, should encourage a return to the historical resurrection argument as typified by Dr. Johnson.

Not infrequently the claim is made that an evidential apologetic is a modern, post-seventeenth century product—a "new rationalism" appealed to as a desperate last stand by Christians faced with modern secular criticism of their beliefs—and that such a defense is fundamentally contrary to the spirit of the Protestant Reformers. Chapter seven shows how very wrong such an allegation is with respect to Luther and to the theology which developed from his rediscovery of the gospel and the Scriptures. Indeed, evidential apologetics turns out to be no less than the epistemological handmaid of genuine Reformation theology.

Passing to the contemporary scene, in chapter eight we offer several concrete examples of the dangers of presuppositionalism. One danger is in the realm of Christian interpretation of technology and science, where factual evidence has to be offered for a world-view if it is to say anything significant in the face of contradictory alternatives. Other illustrations show the danger of modern nonevangelical theology, where liberal varieties of "invincible ignorance" have virtually toppled the queen of the sciences from the throne she once occupied by refusing any ultimate testability for religious views.

Chapter nine argues that there is a necessary interrelation between Christian faith and communication. It is an inherent relationship stemming from the objective nature of God's revelatory contact with man through His Word (in the twofold sense of the Lord Christ and the Holy Scriptures). Indeed, it is this very objective communication that makes possible the factual, evidential case for Christianity.

The final chapter lays great stress on the need, both in theology and in the defense of the faith, to maintain the objective, factually inerrant character of the Bible. The "battle for the Bible" reveals itself to be not just an ecclesiastical battle but also an apologetic struggle upon which nothing less than the credibility of historic Christianity rests. Lose the Bible and you lose the best evidence for God; defend the Bible and you discover "many infallible proofs" for the salvation revealed once for all through the death and resurrection of His Son (Acts 1:3).

In sum, the present volume offers essays in *meta-apologetics:* essays that can help the reader to choose an apologetic method capable of withstanding the onslaughts of modern unbelief and of shifting the ground from defense to attack. The essence of this method is never to be satisfied with the mere assertion of Christian truth (since anyone can make claims), or with the critical destruction of a non-Christian viewpoint (since the fallaciousness of another world-view never establishes the truth of your own), but rather to show the secularist that Christianity alone can offer adequate factual, evidential support for its beliefs.

Christian faith *is* founded on fact. The message of this book is simply that the time is now more than ripe for the church to present that faith evidentially and cou-rageously.

John Warwick Montgomery

Strasbourg, France
5 June 1977
The Festival of the Holy Trinity

Acknowledgments

Some (but not all) of the essays contained in the book have previously appeared in print, either in journals or in other hard-to-find locations—such as a Swedish Festschrift! Opportunity has been afforded here to make minor corrections and additions to these essays, and the author thanks the original publishers for their courtesy in permitting wider dissemination of his material.

"The Place of Reason in Christian Witness": *HIS Magazine* [Inter-Varsity Christian Fellowship], February and March, 1966; *Lutheran Synod Quarterly*, Vol. 11, No. 1 (special issue), Fall, 1970 (under the title: "Should Christianity Be Defended?").

"Are You Having a Fuddled Easter?": *Christianity Today*, March 31, 1972; *Melodyland: An International Magazine*, Vol. 1, No. 1 April–May, 1977 (condensed under the title, "Erasing Easter Errors").

"How Muslims Do Apologetics": (*Muslim World*, Vol. 51, No. 2, April, 1961, with author's "Corrigendum" in the July, 1961 *Muslim World*.

"Dr. Johnson As Apologist": *Christianity Today*, April 15, 1977.

"One Upon an A Priori": *Jerusalem and Athens: Critical Discussions on the Theology and Apologetics of Cornelius Van Til*, ed. E. R. Geehan (Philadelphia: Presbyterian and Reformed Publishing Co., 1971), pp. 380–92, 482–83 (Van Til's response follows on pp. 392–403, 483–84).

"Lutheran Theology and the Defense of Biblical Faith": *Ditt Ord Är Sanning: En Handbok om Bibeln, tillägnad David Hedegaard,* ed. Seth Erlandsson ("Biblicums Skriftserie," Nr. 2; Uppsala: Stiftelsen Biblicum/ Bökförlaget Pro Veritate, 1971), pp. 234–58 (in Swedish, under the title, "Bibeln och dess försvar"); *Lutheran Synod Quarterly,* Vol. 9, No. 1 (special issue), Fall, 1970.

Essays representing "The Current Scene": *Christianity Today,* June 23, 1972; Sept. 29, 1972; March 16, 1973, May 9, 1975; Nov. 7, 1975; Jan. 30, 1976.

"Mass Communication and Scriptural Proclamation": *The Evangelical Quarterly* [England], Vol. 49, No. 1, Jan.–Mar., 1977.

"Whither Biblical Inerrancy": *Christianity Today,* July 29, 1977, pp. 40–42.

The appendix first appeared in *Christianity Today* under "Survey of Evangelical Apologetes," April 1, 1977, p. 46.

Introduction
CAN FAITH REST ON FACT?

The theme uniting and justifying this collection of apologetic essays is the compelling facticity of Christian argument. But the moment such a claim is asserted, voices are raised—within the evangelical community itself, remarkably enough—against the possibility of making a factual case for Christian truth. Faith cannot be founded on fact, we are told, even if the facts are really there. The crucial nature of this issue warrants a brief introductory examination of the latest attempt to bypass evidential apologetics: Carl F.H. Henry's *God, Revelation and Authority*.[1] The first two volumes of Henry's work make repeated negative reference to the position espoused by this writer as to the "self-interpreting" character of Christian evidence. Readers of this book should more thoroughly understand and appreciate its significance against the backdrop of Henry's alternative.

Henry offers no original evangelical philosophy, *Time* magazine notwithstanding. With minor variants, he advocates the apriorism long met with in the orthodox Calvinist writings of his generation: Gordon Clark, Cornelius Van Til, and Herman Dooyeweerd.[2]

---

[1]Published by Word Books, Waco, Texas, 1976; references to volume and page numbers will be cited within the text.

[2]Readers may enjoy comparing my ("confessional") and Henry's ("evangelical") answers to the same series of theological questions in Robert Campbell, O. P. (ed.), *Spectrum of Protestant Beliefs* (Milwaukee: Bruce, 1968), *passim*.

Though uncomfortable with the most consistent form of "revelational presuppositionalism," which holds that even laws of logic have no justification apart from special revelation (Vol. 1, p. 236), he follows the main presuppositionalist line in rejecting empirical verifiability and falsifiability (Vol. 1, pp. 96–111). He rejects any and all use of "an experiential criterion for validating theology" (Vol. 1, p. 237), even in the semi-presuppositionalist manner of Edward John Carnell.

To slow his meteoric descent into the abyss of fideism, Henry claims that "logical consistency is a negative test of truth and coherence a subordinate test" (Vol. 1, p. 232), that is, that the Christian position alone is free from logical contradiction and offers the most coherent explanation of universal phenomena.

> How shall the unbeliever recognize the superiority of Christian claims if the logical weaknesses of his alternative are not exposed, and the superiority of revelational truth in confronting the basic issues of reality and life are not exhibited? . . . . It [Christianity] embraces knowledge of the ultimate world and anticipates man's future destiny. It exhibits the wonder of the cosmos, the meaning and worth of individual existence . . . (Vol. 1, p. 238).

What might appear to be given to the non-Christian with one hand (a neutral opportunity to determine whether Christianity does actually fit "reality and life" better than alternative world-views) is, however, immediately taken away with the other, since Henry never tires of repeating that only revelation can put facts into proper perspective. Henry claims the non-Christian cannot be expected to judge factual evidence rightly from his sinful and falsely autonomous perspective.

Thus Henry's demonstrations of the superiority of the Christian view reduce to little more than circular declarations that other positions are less "rational" or less "internally consistent." For example, the process thought of Schubert Ogden (who, not so incidentally, decimated Henry in a dialogue on the subject some years ago at the Trinity Evangelical Divinity School) is dispensed as being "neither as comprehensive nor as consistent as historic Christian theism which speaks of God only in view of His rational self-disclosure and links man to his Maker because of a rationally significant divine image through which God addresses him both in general revelation and in scripturally revealed truths. The alternatives to biblical theism sooner or later break down through their forfeiture of internal consistency" (Vol. 1, p. 408). Few non-Christians will be impressed by arguments of this genre in which the Christian stacks the deck by first defining "rationality" and "internal consistency" in terms of the content of his own revelational position and then judges all other positions by that self-serving criterion.

But we need not discuss here the overall debility of presuppositional orientations; sufficient material on that subject is interspersed throughout the following chapters. What we do wish to speak to at the outset is Henry's pronunciamento that empirical facts—and in particular historical facts—are incapable of establishing the Christian case.

He tells us that "at most an empirical test can indicate whether religious beliefs have a perceptually discernible significance. It cannot at all decide the objective meaning or existence of the supraempirical" (Vol. 1, p. 262). He claims that "no amount of historical inquiry can prove that Jesus is the Christ" (Vol. 2, p. 315). What "perceptually discernible significance" may or may not signify here is entirely unclear. It appears to be a weasel expression required because Henry can hardly bring himself to say that empirical reality has *no* inherent, brute impact on non-Christian and Christian alike. But to deny that the empirical evidence in behalf of the claims of Jesus can and does simultaneously give us "many infallible proofs" as to the Godhead He manifested is to miss the very reality of the Incarnation. When God became incarnate, the "supraempirical" became empirical, thereby giving us opportunity to meet the Deity by way of the humanity of Jesus. The primary documents concerning Jesus' prophetically foretold and miraculous career will not permit an acceptance of Him as a mere man; he who by means of the testimony of eyewitnesses has seen Him has concurrently and demonstrably also seen the Father. The evidence in that regard is unequivocal. Either reject those documents outright (requiring a rejection of primary historical documentation in general) or accept a Jesus who is both man *and* "supraempirical" God and Savior. If you reject Him it will not be because of a deficiency of evidence but because of a perversity of will, leading, as J.R.R. Tolkien has so well observed, "to sadness or to wrath."

Henry argues that the New Testament "miracle manifestations are not currently at our disposal," that "unlike the natural scientist the historian cannot repeat experiments under controlled conditions," and that even contemporary historical data such as those related to Kennedy's assassination are too unclear to permit definite conclusions (Vol. 1, pp. 261–62; Vol. 2, p. 322ff). But although repeatability is helpful, it is not in any way essential to the establishment of factual truth (your school experiences are not repeatable, but presumably you know that you *had* them), and historical research is perfectly able to determine, for example, that Lincoln was shot in Ford's Theater and did not fatally slip on a banana peel in Peoria. The resurrection of Jesus Christ is in principle no less historically knowable. Henry, in company with many philosophers and journalists who are untrained and inexperienced in actual historical research, overlooks what actually constitutes evidential sufficiency in determining that given past events have in fact occurred.

Henry casts doubt on the efficacy of the historical case for Jesus' claims because we cannot "marshal impressive independent empirical data outside the New Testament narratives to confirm the intricate web of events reported in the Gospels" (Vol. 1, p. 258). But whether the data are "inside" or "outside" the New Testament is irrelevant; what is relevant is the primary-source quality of those data. Indeed, one of the major reasons the books comprising the New Testament today arrived there in the first place was their primary-source character. The early church accepted them because they were found to be written by apostles or derived from apostolic circles.

"Must one not appeal rather," opines Henry, "to rational consistency than simply to historical method in order to establish the validity of the Gospel portrait?" We reply, just ask your friendly neighborhood historian whether or not "rational consistency" is the way to validate portraits!

But Henry's paramount argument is that "empirical data are always marshaled in the interest of a given perspective. There cannot even be a 'datum' or fact except as defined by a theory" (Vol. 1, p. 259).

> The historical redemptive acts are no more self-interpreting than are other historical acts, and their factuality cannot be defended apart from their divinely given meaning. . . . Empirical probability can indeed be combined with inner certainty when the meaning of specific happenings is transcendently vouchsafed, that is, when that meaning is objectively given by divine revelation. . . . Christian faith requires not simply the redemptive historical act but its meaning or significance as well; historical research alone is impotent either to guarantee any past event or to adduce its meaning or theological import (Vol. 2, p. 330).

Here we have it: faith cannot be founded on fact, for "fact" gains factual status and significance only from its inclusion in a revelational context, which (to be sure) cannot itself be factually justified! Henry rejects any notion of "self-interpreting" facts. He contends that even if facts were historically demonstrable, their meanings would have to be provided by undemonstrable revelation.

This dichotomy between fact and meaning is, if possible, even more unrealistic than Henry's lack of confidence in historical investigation. Facts are not made of wax, capable of infinite molding from the pressure of interpretive world-views. Even Thomas Kuhn, who attempted (not too successfully) in his *Structure of Scientific Revolutions* to show that changes in scientific perspective are largely determined by metaphysical and cultural factors, has to admit that in the last analysis the factual results of "crucial experiments" can sound the death knell of an older theory and the enthronement of its replacement.[3] Facts ultimately arbitrate interpretations, not the reverse, at least where good science (and not bad philosophy) is being practiced.

Chapter 2 of this present work shows specifically how historically established resurrection fact requires the interpretation that Jesus rose because of His deity. Other interpretations, when brought to the bar of this fact, fall by the wayside because they cannot adequately account for the data. Had Henry assimilated my essay "The Theologian's Craft" in *The Suicide of Christian Theology*, he would have benefited from a close analysis of how facts determine interpretive constructs in Christian theology no less than in secular science.

If one removes his nose from philosophical speculation

---

[3]Thomas S. Kuhn, *The Structure of Scientific Revolutions* (Chicago: University of Chicago Press, Phoenix Books, 1964), pp. 152–53.

and breathes the fresher air of societal and personal
decision-making, he will find abundant illustration that
facts must carry their own interpretations (i.e., must arbitrate among diverse interpretations of the data). In the
law, for example, the very possibility of justly deciding
societal conflicts on the basis of factual evidence is dependent on the ability of facts to speak for themselves.
Thus the U. S. Supreme Court, in the famous "second
Williams' case," established that a divorce on substituted
or constructive service in one state need only be given full
faith and credit by another state when the parties have
acquired a bona fide domicile in the divorcing state. The
Court wrote:

> Petitioners, long time residents of North Carolina, came to
> Nevada, where they stayed in an auto-court for transients,
> filed suits for divorce as soon as the Nevada law permit-
> ted, married one another as soon as the divorces were
> obtained, and promptly returned to North Carolina to live.
> *It cannot reasonably be claimed that one set of inferences*
> *rather than another regarding the acquisition by peti-*
> *tioners of new domicils in Nevada could be drawn from*
> *the circumstances attending their Nevada divorces.* (Wil-
> liams v. North Carolina, 325 U. S. 226, 65 Sup. Ct. 1092,
> 157 A. L. P. 1366; italics mine.)

Just where would crucial decision-making in law, history,
or ordinary life arrive if facts could not be relied upon to
yield the appropriate "set of inferences" for their interpretation?

Or consider playwright Harold Pinter's response to a
theatergoer who did not believe that the events of Pinter's
play were self-interpreting:

> Dear Sir:
>
> I would be obliged if you would kindly explain to me the
> meaning of your play "The Birthday Party." These are the
> points which I do not understand:

1—Who are the two men?
2—Where did Stanley come from?
3—Were they all supposed to be normal?
You will appreciate that without the answers to my questions, I cannot fully understand your play.

Yours faithfully,
Mrs. _____

Dear Madam:

I would be obliged if you would kindly explain to me the meaning of your letter. These are the points which I do not understand:
1—Who are you?
2—Where do you come from?
3—Are you supposed to be normal?
You will appreciate that without the answers to my questions, I cannot fully understand your letter.

Yours faithfully,
HAROLD PINTER

Pinter here delightfully drives home the point that if events are not self-interpreting, the inevitable consequence is an infinite regress to absurdity. And such a regress cannot be halted by a gratuitous appeal to "divinely given meaning."

We leave aside Henry's badly confused presentation of my philosophy of history (Vol. 1, p. 256–59)—a fault which could easily have been remedied (1) by reading more of my work and in particular some of the articles now collected in the present book; (2) by consulting the *latest* editions of my publications, such as the second edition of *The Shape of the Past*, with Dr. Paul Feinberg's keen philosophical defense of his evidential apologetic; (3) by reading more slowly and carefully what he did read; and (4) by discussing my position with me personally. He never did this, although for two years while he was writing his work I lived only fifteen minutes from him (he in Arlington and I in Falls Church, Virginia).

The point at issue does not require belaboring: readers of this book need not return to a nineteenth-century aprioristic religious metaphysic at a time when philosophy itself has made tremendous strides in the direction of truth-testing and verification. One can confidently rely on fact to support faith. The privilege and responsibility exist to employ facts to lead today's seeking unbeliever to the faith once delivered to the saints.

1

The Place of Reason in Christian Witness*

A series of lectures I gave at the University of British Columbia on the historical truth of the Christian faith[1] brought a number of appreciative letters and two others. The two correspondents were both troubled by the same thing: my apparent endeavor to *prove* Christianity to the non-Christian. One of the students, from Göttingen University, Germany, wrote: "When one sets out to prove the validity of the Christian religion, there is no longer a place for faith. Faith is commitment, not to what can be made easy to swallow by sane arguments, but to that radical voice which calls directly to us, 'I am the resurrection, and the life: . . . whosoever liveth and believeth in me shall never die' (John 11:25, 26)."

---

*The 1970 Reformation Lectures at Bethany Lutheran College, Mankato, Minnesota.

[1]Published as chaps. 2 and 3 in the author's *Where Is History Going?*, reprint ed. (Minneapolis: Bethany, 1972), pp. 37–74.

In these words, the Göttingen student expresses a tension between reason and faith, between knowing and believing, between head knowledge and heart commitment. So important is this issue for Christians in our secular age, it warrants the most detailed analysis. First, I shall examine the most important negative criticisms frequently voiced against "defending the faith"; then I will suggest biblical justification for the necessity of apologetics.

UNDER FIRE

Apologetics, that branch of theology concerned with the defense of the Christian truth, has fallen on hard times. Though traditionally considered one of the three major branches of systematic theology, it is hardly represented at all in seminary curricula today. In light of the conflicts among liberals, neoorthodox, and orthodox, one would expect that apologetics would have vociferous champions as well as opponents, but the surprising fact is that few theologians of any stripe show any real interest. Quite the contrary. Across the theological spectrum apologetics is viewed with a distinctly jaundiced eye. A person like C. S. Lewis contrasts like the proverbial sore thumb with the numerous theologians who, though they have difficulty agreeing on much else, unite in their opposition to "proving Christianity." Let us examine briefly but critically the attitude of three major theological positions in this matter; after doing so, we will be in a good position to discover why so much of present-day Christendom finds it difficult to "give an answer to every man that asketh you a reason of the hope that is in you" (1 Pet. 3:15).

PROTESTANT MODERNISM

Liberalism's displeasure with efforts to defend Christianity was made explicit by Willard L. Sperry in his book, "*Yes, But—*": *The Bankruptcy of Apologetics* (1931). For Sperry and the modernism he represented, Christians who argued for biblical truth over against scientific judgments were hopelessly deluded. When science spoke, theology was to listen; and in cases where biblical statements seemed to be contradicted by scientific opinion, the former ought properly to be rejected or recast in scientifically accommodating terms.

Two basic assumptions underlay Sperry's argument. First, he maintained the modernist position that Christianity is basically not a religion of propositional, objective truth, but rather a way of life focusing on subjective feeling *(Schleiermacher)* and moral action (the "social gospel"). Thus the defense of doctrine was beside the point; science is the source of cognitive data about the world, and theology should bow to its judgments. Second, Sperry believed that Christianity was not qualitatively different from other religions of the world. Since all religious roads lead up the mountain of truth, one should not try to convince others of Christianity's special claims.

The fallacy of the modernist view of Christianity is now generally recognized in theological circles. The New Testament most definitely presents the Christian faith as a matter of concrete, cognitive truth. Whether one looks at Christ's demands ("Believe me that I am in the Father, and the Father in me"—John 14:11) or at the explicit creedal affirmations of the apostles ("I delivered unto you first of all that which I also received, how that Christ died for our sins according to the scriptures . . . and that he rose again the third day according to the scriptures"—1 Cor. 15:3, 4), one sees that Christianity is not primarily a matter of feeling or even of action, but a religion of factual belief—factual belief that yields genuine religious experience and meaningful social action, only because of its objective truth. Moreover, contrary to liberal theology, the Christianity of the New Testament is presented as qualitatively different from all other religions, past or future. "I am the way, the truth, and the life: no man cometh unto the Father, but by me," said Jesus (John 14:6); "there is none other name under heaven given among men, whereby we must be saved," His apostles preached (Acts 4:12).

Thus modernism's opposition to apologetics falls to the ground, for it is based on a misunderstanding of the nature of Christianity itself. A nonfactual religion, of course, is not capable of factual defense; but Christianity, grounded in the fact of God's entrance into human history in the person of Christ, is the factual and defensible religion *par excellence*.

BARTH AND BULTMANN

Though Karl Barth was largely responsible for the demise of modernism, his displeasure with attempts to defend Christianity was as great as that of the modernists. True, he firmly maintained the objective factual character of the saving events in Scripture (the incarnation, death, and resurrection of our Lord, etc.), and he proclaimed these events as unique and Christianity as the final religious truth.

But the impact of Barth's return to the Bible has been considerably weakened by his efforts to remove the key events of the plan of salvation from secular examination. Early in his career he asserted that the miraculous events of the gospel (virgin birth, resurrection, etc.) took place in a "meta-historical" or "suprahistorical" realm *(Geschichte)*—a realm not subject to the canons of ordinary historical *(historische)* investigation.[2] In his later writings he preferred not to make this distinction between

---

[2]See Montgomery, "Karl Barth and Contemporary Theology of History," *Where Is History Going?*, pp. 100–117.

realms of history, but he still affirmed that the miraculous events of Scripture cannot be validated apart from prior belief in them.[3] Consistent with this approach, Barth held that neither the Bible itself nor the saving events recorded in it can be objects of "proof" to the unbeliever; it is only by faith that the Bible assumes its functions as God's Word in a man's life.

Rudolf Bultmann and his followers have removed Christian truth even farther from objective verification. For them, the essence of the Christian message does not lie in historical accounts of Christ's miraculous saving activity. Biblical miracles are either denied outright or regarded as meaningless and therefore irrelevant to modern man. The New Testament accounts of Christ are "demythologized" so as to yield their "true" core: the existential experience of salvation. Christianity then becomes the proclamation of existential experience of salvation in the present, not a defense of supposedly objective truth in the past. Truth is known only in "personal encounter" with the Christ of faith, and efforts to shift attention to rational proofs are to be rejected as religiously and psychologically unrealistic.[4]

Both Barth and Bultmann unhappily share modernism's conviction that objective, factual investigation of the Bible will destroy traditional belief in its truthfulness. For Barth this has meant the walling off of salvation events from historical scrutiny and for Bultmann, the desertion of objective, historical truth for subjective, psychological conviction. But the Scripture asserts without qualification that "the Word was made flesh" (John 1:14),

---

[3]Cf. my remarks in "Faith, History, and the Resurrection," *Where Is History Going?*, pp. 225–39.

[4]On Bultmann's existential philosophy of history, see Montgomery, *The Shape of the Past*, 2nd ed. (Minneapolis: Bethany, 1975), pp. 120–22.

that the factual character of the Resurrection could convince even the faithless (John 20:24–29), and that "none of these things" (Christ's saving work and miracles) were hidden or done in a corner (Acts 26:26). In actual fact, it is not the defense of the gospel that makes God's truth irrelevant, but the refusal to defend it in the objective terms of the New Testament proclamation.[5]

MISGUIDED ORTHODOXY

Some Christians, though thoroughly opposed to contemporary dilutions of the gospel message, have joined the hew and cry against defending the faith. Two varieties of orthodox opposition to apologetics can be singled out: the presuppositionalist and the fideist. Doubtless our Göttingen student represents one or the other, if not both, of these viewpoints.

For the orthodox presuppositionalist, a radical break exists between the worlds of the Christian and the non-Christian—a cleavage so fundamental that the Christian cannot convince the non-Christian of Christian truth. Some presuppositionalists argue that non-Christians cannot even discover secular facts; others, that non-Christians, though they can determine secular facts apart from faith, cannot interpret them rightly; and still others, that the non-Christian, even if he can be led to revelational facts, will not interpret them properly when he does meet them. But all presuppositionalists, whether of a strict or mild variety, are convinced that the non-Christian is incapable of arriving at a proper interpretation of saving truth. From this, it follows that the Christian is attempting the impossible if he tries apologetically to persuade the non-

---

[5]Cf. my report of Barth's lectures at the University of Chicago in 1962: "Barth in Chicago: Kerygmatic Strength and Epistemological Weakness," In Montgomery, *The Suicide of Christian Theology* (Minneapolis: Bethany, 1970), pp. 191–93.

Christian of the objective truthfulness of the Gospel account. The non-Christian lives in his presuppositional
world and the Christian in his; and no amount of rational
argument can break down the wall between them.

The fideist goes even farther. He says that not only is it
intellectually impossible to convince the unbeliever of the
truth of Christianity; it is unspiritual to try. Only God
convinces men of Christianity's veracity, and you or I can
do no more than preach His gospel. To endeavor to argue
with the unbeliever is to substitute human wisdom for the
Spirit's working (1 Cor. 1), and thus misunderstand the
depth of human depravity and of man's need to rely solely
on God.

Our answer to these orthodox objections to apologetics
will necessitate a discussion more detailed than that dealing with liberal and neoorthodox theological positions.
(Note how much deeper the "conservative" objections
strike than do the antiapologetic views of modernism,
neoorthodoxy, and Bultmann's existentialism.) Immediately, however, we can point to essential difficulties
in these "orthodox" views. The presuppositionalist finds
it impossible for non-Christian and Christian to experience common ground in the matter of revelational fact and
interpretation. But consider that in the realm of secular
fact (e.g. the chemical composition of water or the historical crossing of the Rubicon by Caesar), both Christian and
non-Christian are capable of discovering truth and interpreting it. All university life is predicated on this assumption, and advances in human knowledge are indisputable
evidence that even unregenerate man can understand the
factual nature of the world and rationally interpret the
data of his experience.

Now if we say that the events of Christ's life (or the
biblical events in general) are not subject to comparable
treatment, then whether we like it or not we are actually

divorcing "Christian facts" from secular, nonreligious facts. Yet this is precisely what the Incarnation denies! In Christ, God truly entered the human sphere. And if this is the case, the human events of His life objectively display His deity and are not adequately explainable apart from it. Such factual and interpretive conclusions will certainly arise when Jesus' life is subjected to the investigative techniques applied to other historical events—provided, of course, that unempirical bias (e.g. against the possibility of the miraculous) is not allowed to distort the documentary picture. Thus, Christ's resurrection can be examined by non-Christians as well as by Christians. Its factual character, when considered in light of the claims of the One raised from the dead, points not to a multiplicity of equally possible interpretations, but to a single "best" interpretation (to an interpretation most consistent with the data), namely the deity of Christ (John 2:18–22).

Of course, sinful self-interest may tempt the non-Christian to avoid the weight of evidence, just as self-interest has so frequently corrupted investigation in other purely secular matters. But selfish perversions of data or interpretation can be made plain in the area of revelational fact no less than in the nonrevelational sphere, for Christian revelation occurred in time—in the secular world. To miss this point is to miss the character of the Incarnation. God came to earth and by manifold proofs showed Himself to men. We do Him and our fellowmen a disservice when we imply that His presence among us was a docetic phantasm, open only to the subjective eye of faith and not to objective examination by every seeker for truth.

Yet are we not unspiritually arrogating to human reason a work that only God's Word and Holy Spirit can perform? Hardly, when it is God's Word that records the historical facts and offers the soundest historical interpretations relating to Christ's gospel. As for the Spirit, He works through that very Word to convince men of God's truth, so that in reality we bring men under His convicting aegis as we point them to the biblical evidences for Christ's truth. More, however, needs to be said by way of a specific examination of the scriptural mandates for defending the faith.

TRUTH AND THE NEW TESTAMENT

In the deepest sense, the Bible identifies truth with the person of Jesus Christ, the God-man who came to earth to die for the sins of the world (John 14:6). Thus, knowing the truth ultimately depends on one's personal relationship to Christ: "If you continue in my [Christ's] word, then you are indeed my disciples, and you shall know the truth, and the truth shall make you free" (John 8:31, 32).

But the question immediately arises, What of those who hesitate to enter such a personal relationship because they doubt the validity of Jesus' claims? Are they to be regarded as dishonest persons endeavoring to hide willful opposition to Christ under the cloak of alleged intellectual doubts? If so, we would expect them to receive little mercy in the New Testament. Like the hypocritical Pharisees, they ought to be condemned as "whited sepulchres" that they might be brought to their senses and to a recognition of their moral perversity.

But this is not the case. Let's consider the key example of Thomas, whose confrontation with the risen Christ forms a climactic event in John's Gospel.[6] In John 20:24–29, just prior to the apostle's explanation of his purpose for writing his book, Thomas is presented as one who would not believe the other disciples' testimonies that they had seen the resurrected Christ. From this, the con-

---

[6]Cf. Montgomery, "The Fourth Gospel Yesterday and Today", *The Suicide of Christian Theology*, pp. 428–65.

clusion is inescapable that in spite of his contact with Jesus during His earthly ministry, Thomas had not yet become a Christian, since belief in the Resurrection is an essential element in the gospel (Rom. 4:23–25; 1 Cor. 15). Thomas demanded concrete, empirical proof of Jesus' claim to rise again after three days. He would not be convinced, he said, unless he could put his finger into Jesus' nailprints and thrust his hand into the wound made when Jesus' side was pierced.

And what did Jesus do? Did He reject Thomas's demand for objective proof on the ground (so often used by opponents of apologetics) that such demands are really sinful cover-ups for willful refusal to believe? Not at all. Jesus appeared to Thomas and provided him with exactly the empirical evidence that he needed to become convinced of His deity. Thomas's cry, "My Lord and my God," is perhaps the strongest confession of Jesus' divinity in the entire Bible. It was spoken because our Lord was willing, in His grace, specifically to satisfy Thomas's need for concrete evidence that He had risen from the dead.

Though Christ told Thomas that it would have been better for him to have believed without seeing (i.e., that he should have believed the testimonies of his fellow disciples who had already seen the Lord), this rebuke was not given as a substitute for the proof Thomas needed. Rather, it followed both Jesus' appearance to Thomas and Thomas's affirmation of Jesus' deity. Only after Jesus brought Thomas to faith through graciously giving him evidence of His resurrection did He point out to him where his faith had been lacking.

Paul's Areopagus address in Acts 17 gives another clear example that in the New Testament the honest intellectual problems of unbelievers are respected and dealt with on their own ground. At Athens, the apostle confronted Epicurean and Stoic philosophers. The cynical and self-indulgent Epicureans, whom E. M. Blaiklock has called the Sadducees among the Greeks, were not Paul's focus of attention.[7] It is noteworthy that Paul's divine Master also had little patience with the intellectually dishonest Sadducees of Israel (cf. Matt. 22:29, 34). But with the ethically sensitive Stoics it was different. In order to witness effectively to them, Paul began where they were: with their superstitious belief in an unknown god. Through an appeal to truths expressed by their own poets (Paul quotes Stoic sentiments found in Cleanthes, Aratus, and Epimenides), he called for repentance and proclaimed judgment of the world "in righteousness by that man [Jesus] whom he [God] hath ordained; whereof he hath given assurance unto all men, in that he hath raised him from the dead" (Acts 17:31).

Here we have one of the best New Testament examples of missionary and apologetic skill. "He who as a missionary will test the various elements in this speech will find that they all produce their effect," wrote missions specialist Steven J. Warneck.[8] Indeed, as Richard Longenecker has emphasized, Paul's concern to be "all things to all men" in order to bring them to a saving knowledge of Christ (1 Cor. 9:22) is the key to his entire ministry. "From the days of the Fathers, Paul's Athenian experience as recorded in Acts 17 has been cited as the illustration of the 'all things to all men' principle as it worked out in the Gentile situation."[9] Like his Lord, Paul

---

[7]Blaiklock, who is professor and chairman emeritus of the department of classics at the University of Auckland, New Zealand, made this point in delivering the Annual Wheaton College Graduate School Lectures, October 21–22, 1964.

[8]Steven J. Warneck, *Paulus im Lichte der heutigen Heidenmission* (1914), pp. 73–74. Cf. Olaf Moe, *The Apostle Paul: His Life and Work,* trans. L.A. Vigness (Minneapolis: Augsburg, 1950), pp. 279–97.

[9]Richard Longenecker, *Paul, Apostle of Liberty* (New York: Harper, 1964), p. 230.

was willing to operate on the unbeliever's own ground. He did not position himself outside the unbeliever's frame of reference and preach at him (Paul Tillich would say, "throw stones at his head"); rather, he literally became all things to all honest seekers, whether Jews or Greeks, so as to bring them to the light of Christ.[10]

How can Jesus and Paul take such an attitude toward truth, an attitude which encourages the believer to enter the non-Christian's frame of reference and convince him that the gospel is veracious? The New Testament does this primarily because, unlike much of contempory theology, it sees the full implications of the Incarnation. If, as we stressed earlier, God *really* became man in Jesus Christ, then His entrance into the human sphere is open to examination by non-Christian and Christian alike, and the honest doubter will find compelling evidence in support of Christ's claims. This is why the New Testament makes so much of the eyewitness contact the early church had with its Lord (cf. 1 John 1:1–4). The church of the New Testament is not an esoteric, occult, gnostic sect whose teachings are demonstrable only to initiates; it is the religion of the incarnate God, at whose death the veil of the temple was rent from top to bottom, opening holy truth to all who would seek it.

APOLOGETIC NEED

The twentieth-century world, growing steadily smaller as the communication revolution continues, displays a

---

[10]On the relation of the Areopagus address to 1 Corinthians 1, F.F. Bruce rightly says: "The popular idea that his [Paul's] determination, when he arrived in Corinth, to know nothing there 'save Jesus Christ, and him crucified,' was the result of disillusionment with the line of approach he had attempted at Athens, has little to commend it" *(Commentary on the Book of Acts* "New International Commentary on the New Testament"; Grand Rapids, Mich.: Eerdmans, 1954, p. 365). See also N.B. Stonehouse, *Paul before the Areopagus* (Grand Rapids, Mich.: Eerdmans, 1957), where this point is made *in extenso.*

religious pluralism experientially unknown to our grand-fathers and remarkably similar to the heterogenous religious situation in the Roman Empire during the first century. Sects and cults proliferate; philosophies of life, explicit and implicit, vie for our attention; and older, previously dormant religions, such as Buddhism and Islam, are engaged in vigorous proselytizing.[11] All about us ultimate concerns spring up, each claiming to be more ultimate, more worthy of our total commitment, than the other. In the university world the pluralistic cacophony is louder than perhaps anywhere else: materialism, idealism, pragmatism, communism, hedonism, mysticism, existentialism, and a hundred other options present themselves to the college student in classrooms, bull-sessions, student organizations, political rallies, and social activities.

What is the non-Christian to do, when amid this din he hears the Christian message? Are we Christians so naive as to think that he will automatically, *ex opere operato,* accept Christianity as true and put away world-views contradicting it? And if we call out to him, "Just try Christianity and you will find that it proves itself experientially," do we really think that he will not at the same time hear precisely the same subjective-pragmatic appeal from numerous other quarters?

What is he to do? Alphabetize the "ultimate concerns" and try them serially? If so, he must at least try agnosticism, atheism, Baha'i, and Buddhism (Mahayana and Hinayana!) before coming to Christianity. In *The God that Failed,* the accounts of Arthur Koestler and others who have extricated themselves painfully from Marxist commitment tell us that movement from one ultimate concern

---

[11]Cf. Montgomery, "How Muslims Do Apologetics" (ch. 4 of the present work).

to another is a psychologically devastating experience.[12]
There is every chance that by the time the non-Christian
comes to try Christianity, he will be so jaded psychologically that he will be incapable of recognizing ultimate truth
when he actually meets it.

Evidently, what is necessary for effective Christian
witness in a pluralistic world is an objective apologetic—a
"reason for the hope that is in you"—that will give the
non-Christian clear ground for experientially trying the
Christian faith before all other options. Absolute proof of
the truth of Christ's claims is available only in personal
relationship with Him; but contemporary man has every
right to expect us to offer solid reasons for making such a
total commitment. The apologetic task is justified not as a
rational substitute for faith, but as a ground for faith; not
as a replacement for the Spirit's working, but as a means
by which the objective truth of God's Word can be made
clear so that men will heed it as the vehicle of the Spirit
who convicts the world through its message.

The analytical philosopher Antony Flew, in developing
a parable from a tale told him by John Wisdom, illustrates
how meaningless to the non-Christian are religious assertions incapable of being tested objectively:

> Once upon a time two explorers came upon a clearing in
> the jungle. In the clearing were growing many flowers and
> many weeds. One explorer says, "Some gardener must
> tend this plot." The other disagrees, "There is no gar-
> dener." So they pitch their tents and set a watch. No
> gardener is ever seen. "But perhaps he is an invisible
> gardener." So they set up a barbed-wire fence. They
> electrify it. They patrol with bloodhounds. (For they re-
> member how H. G. Wells' *The Invisible Man* could be
> both smelt and touched though he could not be seen.) But

---

[12]Arthur Koestler, *et al.*, *The God that Failed*, ed. Richard H. Crossman (New
York: Books for Libraries, 1949).

no shrieks ever suggest that some intruder has received a shock. No movements of the wire ever betray an invisible climber. The bloodhounds never give cry. Yet still the Believer is not convinced. "But there is a gardener, invisible, insensible to electric shocks, a gardener who has no scent and makes no sound, a gardener who comes secretly to look after the garden which he loves." At last the Sceptic despairs, "But what remains of your original assertion? Just how does what you call an invisible, intangible, eternally elusive gardener differ from an imaginary gardener or even from no gardener at all?"[13]

This parable is a damning judgment on all religious truth-claims save that of the Christian faith.[14] For in Christianity we do not have merely an allegation that the garden of this world is tended by a loving Gardener; we have the actual, empirical entrance of the Gardener into the human scene in the person of Christ (cf. John 20:14, 15), and this entrance is verifiable by way of His resurrection.

We must present clear testimony to the Thomases and to the Stoics of our day that God did indeed come in the flesh and "showed himself alive after his passion by many infallible proofs" (Acts 1:3). Under no circumstances should we retreat into a presuppositionalism or a fideism which would rob our fellow men of the opportunity to consider the Christian faith seriously with head as well as heart. Our apologetic task is not fulfilled until we remove the intellectual offenses that allow so many non-Christians to reject the gospel with scarcely a hearing. We must bring them to the only legitimate offense: the offense

[13]Antony Flew, "Theology and Falsification," *New Essays in Philosophical Theology,* ed. Antony Flew and Alasdair MacIntyre (London: SCM Press, 1955), p. 96.

[14]On the issue of theological verification, cf. Montgomery, "Inspiration and Inerrancy: A New Departure," *Crisis in Lutheran Theology,* 2 vols., rev. ed. (Minneapolis: Bethany, 1973), Vol. 1. pp. 15–44.

of the Cross. We must make clear to them beyond a shadow of doubt that if they reject the Lord of glory, it will be by reason of willful refusal to accept His grace, not because His Word is incapable of withstanding the most searching intellectual examination.

When the Greeks of our day come seeking Jesus (John 12:20, 21), let us make certain they find Him.

2

Science, Theology, and the Miraculous*

THE DILEMMA

From earliest Christian history—indeed, from the pages of the Bible itself—miracles have been the mainstay of Christian apologetics. Taking their cue from Jesus' own assertion that the "one sign" to His generation of the truth of His claims would be the "sign of Jonah" (Jesus' resurrection, Matt. 12:39, 40 *et. al.*) and from Paul's catalog of witnesses to that Great Miracle apart from which Christians would be "of all men most miserable" (see 1 Cor. 15), patristic apologists such as Irenaeus, Origen, and Eusebius of Caesarea confidently argued from the historical facticity of our Lord's miracles to the veracity of His claims and the consequent moral obligation to accept

*An invitational presentation at the Lee College Symposium on the Theological Implications of Science (Cleveland, Tennessee) on March 18, 1977.

them.[1] Every major apologist in Christian history from that day to the mid-eighteenth century did likewise, whatever the particular philosophical or theological commitment he espoused. The list includes Augustine the Neo-Platonist, Thomas Aquinas the Aristotelian, Hugo Grotius the Arminian Protestant, Blaise Pascal the Catholic Jansenist, and Joseph Butler the high church Anglican.[2]

But with the onset of modern rationalism in the so-called Enlightenment of the eighteenth century came David Hume's attack on miracle evidence for religious truth-claims. Coupled with Immanuel Kant's critique of the Aristotelian-Thomist theistic proofs for God's existence and Gotthold Lessing's argument that historical data are never certain enough to establish eternal verities, Hume's refutation of the miraculous altered the entire course of Christian apologetics. Indeed, Hume's *Enquiry* can be said without exaggeration to mark the end of the era of classical Christian apologetics.

> Hume's criticism was of course itself immediately subjected to retort and rejoinder. It was only slowly that its devasting character became clear. The end result is to be detected in . . . significant changes in apologetic emphasis and strategy. There is a movement away from presenting prophecy and miracle as external proofs, like flying but-

---

[1]Joseph H. Crehan, "Apologetics," *A Catholic Dictionary of Theology*, Vol. 1 (London: Thomas Nelson, 1962), pp. 113–15; René Aigrain, "Histoire de l'apologétique," *Apologetique*, ed. Brillant and Nédoncelle (Paris: Bloud & Gay, 1937), pp. 950ff.; G.W.H. Lampe, "Miracles and Early Christian Apologetic," *Miracles: Cambridge Studies in Their Philosophy and History*, ed. C.F.D. Moule (London: Mowbray, 1965), pp. 203–18. (Lampe is one of the group known as "Cambridge radicals" and a contributor to Vidler's *Soundings:* his essay must be read in this light.)

[2]Cf. Avery Dulles, *A History of Apologetics* (New York: Corpus; Philadelphia: Westminster Press, 1971), and Bernard Ramm, *Varieties of Christian Apologetics*, rev. ed. (Grand Rapids: Baker Book House, 1961).

tresses, sufficient in themselves to prop up the Christian edifice.[3]

A cruel dilemma thus arises for the modern Christian: far more than his predecessors living in ages of faith he needs to be able to give a reason for his Christian hope, but the chief apologetic support available from miracle evidence seems to be denied him.

CHRISTIAN RESPONSE TO THE DILEMMA AND REBUTTALS TO THE RESPONSE

The overall Christian response to Hume has been terror and flight. Apologists have generally taken their cue from Søren Kierkegaard's willingness to substitute for objective proofs of faith the believer's personal, existential experience and to claim that, in the final analysis, "truth is subjectivity." Thus miracles in the heart have replaced miracles in history in the weaponry not only of theological radicals such as Rudolf Bultmann and neoorthodox advocates of the "theology of crisis," but also of evangelical pietists who sing with A. H. Ackley, "You ask me how I know He lives? He lives within my heart." Unhappily for these positions, however, the analytical philosophy of the twentieth century has devastated attempts to "validate God-talk" by subjective faith experience on the ground that all pure subjectivities are in principle untestable. Their inner truth-claims, being compatible with any and every state of affairs in the external world, are epistemologically meaningless.[4] Miracles in the heart, as I

---

[3]J.K.S. Reid, *Christian Apologetics* (London: Hodder & Stoughton, 1969), p. 156.

[4]See especially Kai Nielsen, "Can Faith Validate God-Talk?" *New Theology No. 1*, ed. Martin Marty and Dean Peerman (New York: Macmillan Paperbacks, 1964); Frederick Ferré, *Language, Logic and God* (New York: Harper, 1961), ch. 8, pp. 94–104; and C.B. Martin, "A Religious Way of Knowing," *New Essays in Philosophical Theology*, ed. Antony Flew and Alasdair MacIntyre (London: SCM Press, 1955).

have noted elsewhere, are philosophically indistinguishable from heartburn, and thus offer little in the way of a
substantial apologetic to modern secularists who have not
yet experienced Jesus Christ personally.[5]

A few modern Christian apologists, recognizing the
defeat inherent in a capitulation to subjectivity, have attempted to persevere along the lines of the classic appeal
to prophecy and miracle. John Henry Newman in the
nineteenth century and C. S. Lewis in the twentieth are
prime examples, and their positive impact should encourage the faint of heart. Lewis—and a respectable number of
contemporary philosophers—have not yielded to Hume;
they have offered trenchant direct attacks on the logic of
his argument against the miraculous.[6] My approach has
followed this same line: I have maintained (1) that when
Hume assumes that there is an "unalterable experience"
against miracles and concludes that miracles do not occur,[7] he is engaged in completely circular reasoning, and
that only a truly inductive approach (examining without
prejudice the firsthand evidence for alleged miracles) can
ever answer the question as to whether they in fact occur [8]; and (2) that miracles cannot be ruled out a priori in
our contemporary Einsteinian universe where, in the
words of philosopher Max Black, the concept of cause is
"a peculiar, unsystematic, and erratic notion," so that
"any attempt to state a 'universal law of causation' must

[5]Montgomery, *The Suicide of Christian Theology* (Minneapolis: Bethany, 1970), pp. 99, 149, 325ff.

[6]C.S. Lewis, *Miracles* (New York: Macmillan, 1947); Bruce Langtry, "Hume on Testimony to the Miraculous," *Sophia* [Australia], Vol. 11, No. 1 (April, 1972), pp. 20–25; Paul Dietle, "On Miracles," *American Philosophical Quarterly*, Vol. 5, No. 2 (April, 1968), pp. 130–34; etc.

[7]David Hume, *An Enquiry Concerning Human Understanding*, Sec. 10, Pt. 1.

[8]Montgomery, *The Shape of the Past*, 2nd ed. (Minneapolis: Bethany, 1975), pp. 288–93.

prove futile."[9] Indeed, the central thrust of my apologetic has been to argue for the compelling nature of Jesus' religious claims on the basis of His deity, and His deity on the basis of the miracle of His resurrection from the dead.[10]

A number of objections to this rehabilitation of the classical miracle-focused apologetic have been raised both within and without the Christian community. The present essay offers an opportunity to reply to them and thereby remove some misconceptions as well as strengthen a case which, I remain convinced, ultimately takes its mandate from biblical revelation itself. We shall not spend any time on the recurrent objection of theological liberals and mediating evangelicals that our case for the biblical miracles involves a naive acceptance of the historicity of the scriptural texts and a neglect of the "assured results of modern criticism." I have pointed out again and again that such "assured results" are nonexistent, that redaction criticism, documentary criticism, and historical-critical method have been weighed in the balance of secular scholarship and found wanting, and that the burden of proof remains on those who want to justify these subjectivistic methods, not on those who take historical documents at face value when their primary-source character can be established by objective determination of authorship and date.[11] We leave this historical issue—which does not really constitute an issue except

[9]Max Black, *Models and Metaphors* (Ithaca, N.Y.: Cornell University Press, 1962), p. 169. See Montgomery, *Where Is History Going?* (Minneapolis: Bethany, 1972), pp. 70–73.

[10]Montgomery, *Where Is History Going?*, pp. 35ff.; *The Shape of the Past*, pp. 138–45; *Christianity for the Toughminded* (Minneapolis: Bethany, 1973), pp. 29–32.

[11]Montgomery, *Crisis in Lutheran Theology*, 2nd ed. (Minneapolis: Bethany, 1973), 2 vols.; *God's Inerrant Word* (Minneapolis: Bethany, 1974).

for those in a modern theological backwater[12]—and proceed to those philosophical criticisms of the miracle-
apologetic which seem to have the greatest force. Five
such criticisms will be dealt with here: (1) Miracles require
law but law negates miracles; (2) The defender of miracles
holds to uniform law while denying it; (3) Miracles even if
provable don't prove deity; (4) Miracles can always be
reduced to natural events, and (5) Science requires us to
reduce miracles to natural events.

"MIRACLES REQUIRE LAW BUT LAW NEGATES MIRACLES"

We are told that we cannot demonstrate a miraculous
occurrence simply by marshaling historical evidence for it
and then making special claims for its significance. For
such an event to be significant, it must contravene natural
law, and so the apologist must first agree to the existence
of uniform law to keep his miracle from becoming trivial;
but the moment he commits himself to absolute natural
law he has perforce ruled out the miracle he wants to
prove! His choice (so the argument goes) is between no
miracle at all or a "miracle" that contravenes no law and
is therefore trivial!

In reply we must first emphasize the point made earlier:
no one (believer or unbeliever) who lives in today's
Einsteinian universe can benefit from the luxury of an
absolute natural law. By this we do not mean to present
the naive argument that the Heisenberg indeterminacy
principle has "negated" Newtonian physics (quantum

[12]Contrast Gerhard Maier, *The End of the Historical-Critical Method*, trans.
Leverenz and Norden (St. Louis: Concordia, 1977); C.S. Lewis, "Modern
Theology and Biblical Criticism," in his *Christian Reflections*, ed. Walter
Hooper (Grand Rapids: Eerdmans, 1967); Adrian N. Sherwin-White, *Roman
Society and Roman Law in the New Testament* (Oxford: Clarendon Press,
1963), especially p. 187.

physics has, rather, introduced a statistical formulation of the same problems);[13] what we are saying is that "abandonment of the deterministic world-view in physics has made it more difficult to regard the existing state of science as finally legislative of what is and what is not possible in nature."[14] Although formulations of natural laws were as subject to the finite limitations of the observer in Newton's day as they are today, the successes of eighteenth-century science bred overconfidence. Hume, drinking deeply at the founts of Newton,[15] transmuted general experience of cosmic regularity (which did and does exist) into "unalterable experience" against miracles (which could not be established even in principle). Today, in the wake of the general and special theories of relativity, there is much less likelihood of scientific or philosophical claims to the "unalterability" of any physical laws.

To be sure, the absence of any meaningful concept of absolute universal law (from the human observer's standpoint) requires the redefinition of what is meant by "miracle." A miracle can no longer be understood as a "violation of natural law," for we are unable to assert that physical laws, being but the generalized product of our observations, are indeed "natural"—that is, absolute and unalterable. R. F. Holland effectively redefines miracle as an event which is (1) empirically certain (actually having occurred), (2) conceptually impossible (inexplicable without appealing beyond our experience), and (3) reli-

---

[13]Cf. Ernst and Marie-Luise Keller, *Miracles in Dispute*, trans. Kohl (Philadelphia: Fortress Press, 1969), pp. 163–76.

[14]Mary Hesse, "Miracles and the Laws of Nature," *Miracles*, ed. Moule, p. 38. See also Werner Schaaffs, *Theology, Physics, and Miracles*, trans. Renfield (Washington, D.C.: Canon Press, 1974).

[15]See R.H. Hurlbutt III, "David Hume and Scientific Theism," *Journal of the History of Ideas*, Vol. 17, No. 4 (October, 1956), pp. 486–97.

gious (calling for a religious explanation).[16] Margaret
Boden simplifies the definition by regarding a miracle as
an event (1) inexplicable in scientific terms but (2) explicable in religious terms.[17] A miracle cannot be viewed
today as a violation of cosmic or physical law; it is best
regarded phenomenally as a *unique, nonanalogous occurrence*. All historical events are unique, and (to para-
phrase George Orwell) some events—such as Napoleon's
career—are more unique than others; but all nonmiraculous historical events, even the most surprising ones, are
analogous to other events in the explanatory patterns we
successfully apply to them. The miracle is both unique
and without analogy (except, of course, insofar as it is
analogous to a similar unexplained miraculous event, as in
the case of the obvious parallel between Jesus' resurrection and Lazarus' resurrection—brought about, not so
incidentally, by Jesus). When compared with nonmiraculous events, the miracle offers a unique, nonanalogous resistance to successful explanation by all the
techniques which would readily account for it if it were
other than miraculous.

To return, however, to our objector's argument. Have
we not fallen into the very trap he set for us? By refusing
to go along with an absolute notion of natural law, have we
not rendered alleged miracles trivial, since they no longer
stand out as a stark violation of cosmic regularity?
Hardly, as the immediately preceding mention of historical uniqueness clearly shows. A historical event does not
need to be miraculous to be significant: significance is a
function of its actual or potential impact on other events

---

[16]R.F. Holland, "The Miraculous," *American Philosophical Quarterly*, Vol. 2,
No. 1 (January, 1965), p. 49.

[17]Margaret A. Boden, "Miracles and Scientific Explanation," *Ratio*, Vol. 11,
No. 2 (December, 1969), p. 138.

and persons (including the observer and student of the event). Thus the battle of Waterloo, though not especially dissimilar to other military engagements in certain respects, is nonetheless of great significance, at least to Englishmen and Frenchmen, because of its effect on their national pride and history. Napoleon's life, with the added dimension of particular historical uniqueness, has even more potential significance—not only for Frenchmen, but also for all those who are fascinated by the wonders of greatness.

Ian Ramsey perceptively observed that scientific regularity tends to reduce rather than heighten significance, whereas history, with its stress on the particular and the concrete, is the stuff out of which significance is made: "Scientific language may detail uniformities more and more comprehensively, but its very success in so doing means that its pictures are more and more outline sketches of concrete, given fact. . . . In history we are not concerned with abstract uniformities but with a *concrete* level of *personal* transactions."[18]

Whether a historical miracle will be "significant," then, will depend not on its relation to supposed natural law, but to its inherent, concrete character. If an event touches the wellsprings of universal human need, its significance can hardly be doubted. And even on the most minimal level, the nonanalogous nature of any miracle serves to attract attention, to raise questions, and perhaps to remind the indifferent of the Socratic truth that the unexamined life is not worth living. Thus does the Scripture refer to even the least redemptive of Jesus' miracles as *semeia*

---

[18]Ian Ramsey, "Miracles: An Exercise in Logical Mapwork," *The Miracles and the Resurrection* ("Theological Collections," 3; London: S.P.C.K., 1964), pp. 7, 13. For my (many) agreements and (some) disagreements with Ramsey's apologetic approach, see Montgomery, *The Suicide of Christian Theology*, pp. 258–60, 278–313.

("signs") that point to Him and to the truth of His divine claims.

"THE DEFENDER OF MIRACLES HOLDS TO UNIFORM LAW WHILE DENYING IT"

Recent opposition to the kind of miracle apologetic I espouse has taken the following sophisticated form in the work of philosopher Antony Flew:

> The basic propositions are: first, that the present relics of the past cannot be interpreted as historical evidence at all, unless we presume that the same fundamental regularities obtained then as still obtain today; second, that in trying as best he may to determine what actually happened the historian must employ as criteria all his present knowledge, or presumed knowledge, of what is probable or improbable, possible or impossible; and, third, that, since *miracle* has to be defined in terms of practical impossibility the application of these criteria inevitably precludes proof of a miracle.[19]

Flew's argument is really two arguments in disguise, and we shall take up each in turn. On the one hand, he seems to be saying that the proponent of miracles has no right to argue for them on the basis of a consistent underlying method of investigation (empirical method), since one cannot assume its absolute regularity and applicability and then use it to prove deviations from regularity. Once a miracle is granted, there would be no reason to consider empirical method as necessarily applicable without exception, so it could perfectly well be inapplicable to the investigation of the miracle claim in the first place!

But here a lamentable confusion is introduced between

---

[19]Antony Flew, *God & Philosophy* (London: Hutchinson, 1966), Sec. 7.10, p. 146.

what may be termed *formal* or *heuristic* regularity and *substantive* regularity. To investigate anything of a factual nature, empirical method must be employed. It involves such formal or heuristic assumptions as the law of non-contradiction, the inferential operations of deduction and induction, and necessary commitments to the existence of the investigator and the external world.[20] Empirical method is not "provable." The justification for its use is the fact that we cannot avoid it when we investigate the world. (To prove that what we perceive with our senses is real, we would have to collect and analyze data in its behalf, but we would then already be using what we are trying to prove!) One cannot emphasize too strongly that this necessary methodology does not in any way commit one to a substantively regular universe: to a universe where events must always follow given patterns. Empirical method always investigates the world in the same way—by collecting and analyzing data—but there is no prior commitment to what the data must turn out to be.

Thus a team of researchers could conceivably go down the rabbit hole with Alice and empirically study even Wonderland, where Alice cried, "Dear, dear! How queer everything is to-day! And yesterday things went on just as usual. I wonder if I've been changed in the night?"[21] Even a world of maximal miracles—where predictability would approach zero—could be investigated by empirical method, for the consistent collection and analysis of data can occur even when the data are not themselves consistent and regular. In short, whereas irregularity in basic

---

[20]See my *Shape of the Past*, pp. 141, 256–67, and my essay, "Clark's Philosophy of History," *The Philosophy of Gordon H. Clark: A Festschrift*, ed. Ronald H. Nash (Philadelphia: Presbyterian and Reformed Publishing Co., 1968), p. 388.

[21]Cf. Peter Heath, ed., *The Philosopher's Alice* (New York: St. Martin's Press, 1974).

empirical methodology would eliminate the investigation
of anything, the discovery of unique, nonanalogous
events by empirical method in no way vitiates its operation or renders the investigator liable to the charge of
irrationality.[22]

Flew has elsewhere expressed a more potent variation
on this same argument in the following terms: the defender of the miraculous is acting arbitrarily when he claims
that "it is (psychologically) impossible that these particular witnesses were lying or misinformed and hence that we
must accept the fact that on this occasion the (biologi-
cally) impossible occurred."[23] The criticism here is that
the advocate of miracles must commit himself to certain
aspects of *substantive* regularity in order to analyze the
evidence for a historical miracle. He must, for example,
assume that human motivations remain the same in order
to argue (as I have) that neither the Romans, the Jewish
religious leaders, nor the disciples would have stolen
Jesus' body in order to claim that Jesus was miraculously
resurrected. But, we are told, such argumentation inconsistently uses regularity of experience where it serves a
purpose and discards it at the point of the desired miracle,
instead of there also insisting on a natural, ordinary explanation.

In reply we might begin by noting that this argument
seems somewhat inappropriate for the rationalist to propose. Since he himself is committed to employ only "ordinary" explanations of phenomena—explanations arising from "common experience"—he is in a particularly
poor position to suggest any abnormal explanations for

---

[22]For the essential similarity between empirical method as applied to the present
and empirical method as applied to past events, see the author's *Shape of the
Past* and *Where Is History Going?*, *passim*.

[23]Antony Flew, "Miracles," *The Encyclopedia of Philosophy*, Vol. 5, ed. Paul
Edwards (New York: Macmillan & The Free Press, 1967), p. 352.

any aspect of a miracle account, including the psychological motivations or responses of the persons involved. Presumably the rationalist would be the last one to appeal to a "miraculous" suspension of ordinary psychology so as to permit the Jewish religious leaders (for example) to have stolen the body of Christ when they knew it to be against their own best interests.

However, the issue lies at a deeper level than this, and we may be able to arrive there by posing the question in the starkest terms. If we interpret or explain historical events along ordinary lines (in accord with ordinary experience) where this does not contradict the events to be interpreted, are we therefore required to conclude that unique, nonanalogous events do not occur even when ordinary observational evidence exists in their behalf? Flew demands that we answer this question in the affirmative. To use common experience of regularities at all in historical interpretation, says he, precludes all possibility of discovering a miracle, even if the use of such common experience provides the very convergence of independent probabilities (as Newman would put it) for asserting that the event in question *is* a miracle.

Curiouser and curiouser, if we may again appeal to Alice! The fallacy in this reasoning arises from a lack of clear perception as to the proper interrelation of the general and the particular in historical investigation. In interpreting events, one's proper goal is to find the interpretation that best fits the facts. Ideally, then, one will set alternative explanations of an event against the facts themselves to make an intelligent choice. But which "facts" will our explanations be tested against—the immediate facts to be interpreted, or the entire, general range of human experience? Where particular experience and general experience are in accord, there is no problem; but where they conflict, the particular must be chosen over the general, for otherwise our "investigations" of historical particulars will be investigations in name only since the results will always reflect already accepted general experience. Unless we are willing to suspend "regular" explanations at the particular points where these explanations are inappropriate to the particular data, we in principle eliminate even the possibility of discovering anything new. In effect, we then limit all new (particular) knowledge to the sphere of already accepted (general) knowledge. The proper approach is just the opposite: the particular must triumph over the general, even when the general has given us immense help in understanding the particular.

In linguistics, for example, our general knowledge of how words function in cognate languages can help us immensely when we want to discover the meaning and function of a word in a new language. In the final analysis, however, only the particular usage of the word in *that* language will be decisive on the question, and where general semantics or lexicography is in tension with particular usage, the latter must triumph over the former. But who would say that the linguist therefore has no right to use general linguistics since he ultimately is willing to subordinate it and revise it on the basis of isolated, particular usage? He would in fact be abrogating his role as linguist if he did allow the general to swallow up the particular at the point of tension between them. Likewise, in the investigation of unique, nonanalogous events (miracles), one has every right to employ regular experience in testing out such claims, but no right to destroy the uniqueness of the event by forcing it to conform to general regularities.

How does a historian properly determine what has occurred and interpret it? Admittedly, he takes to a study of any particular event his fund of general, "usual" experience. He relies upon it wherever it serves a useful function and not because he has any eternal, metaphysical justification for doing so. But the moment the general runs into tension with the particular, the general must yield, since (1) the historian's knowledge of the general is never complete, so he can never be sure he ought to rule out an event or an interpretation simply because it is new to him, and (2) he must always guard against obliterating the uniqueness of individual historical events by forcing them into a Procrustean bed of regular, general patterns. Only the primary-source evidence for an event can ultimately determine whether it occurred or not, and only that same evidence will establish the proper interpretation of the event.

Thus, in the argument for Christ's resurrection, nothing in the primary documents forces the historian to miraculous explanations of motives or actions of the Romans, the Jewish religious leaders, or the disciples (indeed, the documents show them to have acted with exemplary normality—as typically sinful and insensitive members of a fallen race). But these same primary documents do force us to a miraculous understanding of the Resurrection, since any alternative explanation runs directly counter to all of the primary-source facts at our disposal. The documents, in short, force us to go against biological generalizations as to corpses remaining dead, but do not require us to deviate from psychological generalizations as to individual and crowd behavior. Contrary to what Flew imagines, we do not arbitrarily prefer biological miracles over psychological miracles; we accept no miracles unless the primary evidence compels us to it, and if that evidence requires psychological miracles rather than biological ones, we would go that route.[24]

French judge Jacques Batigne describes a bizarre case

---

[24]Montgomery, *Principalities and Powers: The World of the Occult,* 2nd ed. (Minneapolis: Bethany, 1975).

in which a corrupt magistrate's clerk, in the face of overwhelming scientific proof of his guilt, stubbornly maintained his innocence for almost a year, even when it was
unquestionably in his best interest to come clean and he
knew it. Those involved in the case were so impressed by
the clerk's fine past record and sincerity that they did
everything possible to believe that a "physical miracle"
accounted for the evidence against him, but the facts
finally brought them to the conclusion that the "miracle"
was psychological: the clerk inexplicably preferred to act
against his own interest.[25]

The Gospel narratives give us no such situation. There a
biological miracle is forced upon us, like it or not. The
primary facts, and those facts alone, can arbitrate such
questions; generalizations, though helpful to us in reaching the point of primary investigation, must bow to the
facts there revealed.

"MIRACLES EVEN IF PROVABLE
DON'T PROVE DEITY"

Opponents of a miracle apologetic argue that a
proven miracle—even the miracle of Christ's
resurrection—would be vacuous, for it still would not
require belief in God. This viewpoint is held by those
opposing miracles, but even a philosopher who is at
pains to show their epistemological meaningfulness
makes the assertion:

The fact that theological underpinnings are necessary to
the very identification of a miracle in the first place is, of
course, one reason why miracles could never be regarded
as a proof of the existence of some god or God to an
unbeliever who was aware of the various *different* super-

---

[25]Jacques Batigne, *Assignment in Marseilles* (New York: Hart, 1974),
pp. 56–70.

natural powers which could in principle be invoked as explanations of scientifically anomalous events.[26]

Often the claim that "miracles can't prove God" is little more than a variation on Lessing's theme that "the accidental truths of history can never become the proof of necessary truths of reason." Insofar as the argument proceeds in this fashion, it can easily be disposed of, for Lessing confused what contemporary analytical philosophers term the "synthetic" (factual) and the "analytic" (purely formal) areas of assertion. Only in the analytic realm are "necessary truths" possible—truths about which one can be 100 percent certain. Synthetic evidence, involving probabilities and plausibilities, can never rise to such a level of proof. God-statements do not fall into the analytic realm, unless by "God" we mean only a formal assertion of deductive logic or pure mathematics! However, if by "God" we mean an existent, factual being, then any proof of His existence or statement about Him must lie in the realm of the synthetic; that is, it must be factual in character. In reality, then, *only* "the accidental truths" of historical experience are ever capable of becoming the proof of God's existence! Granted, the proof will never reach 100 percent (faith will have to jump the gap from plausibility to certainty), but such proof is the basis of all our factual decisions in life and cannot be summarily dismissed just because a vital religious question is at issue. Thus Jesus was quite willing to use His miraculous healing of the paralytic to demonstrate (not to analytic certainty but with synthetic persuasiveness) that He could forgive sins and was therefore truly divine (Mark 2:1–12, et. al.).

But how persuasive is such a miraculous demonstration, after all? If I were to grow hair on a billiard ball, would this warrant a claim on my part to deity? Hardly,

---

[26]Boden, "Miracles," pp. 143–44.

and such an illustration brings us back to the point made earlier in this paper that the significance of a miracle depends in the final analysis not on the degree to which it "violates natural law" (whatever such a notion can mean, and I doubt that it can mean much in an Einsteinian age), but on the character of the miracle—specifically whether or not it speaks to universal human need.

Even an event that allows for the full range of secondary causes to explain it can have significant miraculous impact if it operates at the point of man's existential need. Holland offers the example of an express train's sudden stop just ahead of a child on the railroad track, owing to a sudden heart attack experienced by the engineer as a result of an earlier argument with a colleague. Holland perceptively comments on this "coincidence" or "contingency" miracle:

> Unlike the coincidence between the rise of the Ming dynasty and the arrival of the dynasty of Lancaster, the coincidence of the child's presence on the line with the arrival and then the stopping of the train is impressive, significant; not because it is very unusual for trains to be halted in the way this one was, but because the life of a child was imperiled and then, against expectation, preserved. The significance of some coincidences as opposed to others arises from their relation to human needs and hopes and fears, their effects for good or ill upon our lives. So we speak of our luck (fortune, fate, etc.). And the kind of thing that, outside religion, we call luck is in religious parlance the grace of God or a miracle of God. But while the reference here is the same, the meaning is different. The meaning is different in that whatever happens by God's grace or by a miracle is something for which God is thanked or thankable, something which has been or could have been prayed for, something which can be regarded with awe and be taken as a sign or made the subject of a vow (e. g., to go on a pilgrimage).[27]

---

[27]Holland, "The Miraculous," p. 44.

When we turn to the unique, nonanalogous event of the Resurrection, used by Jesus and by classical Christian apologists to attest the claim that "God was in Christ, reconciling the world unto himself" (2 Cor. 5:19), we find a maximally compelling reason to bring God into the picture, namely that this miracle deals effectively with the most fundamental area of man's universal need, the conquest of death.[28] Not just a single child is saved from a railway accident; the entire race is freed from death by Jesus' act and consequent promise that "whoever lives and believes in Me shall never die" (John 11:26) and "because I live you shall live also" (John 14:19).

Philosopher Paul Dietl correctly observes that "to prove the existence of a being who deserves some of the predicates 'God' normally gets would be to go some ways toward proving the existence of *God*" and "when and for whom He did miracles would be evidence as to His character."[29] This is precisely why the Resurrection has led so many to affirm Jesus' deity and why His deity is the proper inferential conclusion from His resurrection. The conquest of death for all men is the very predicate of deity that a race dead in trespasses and sins can most clearly recognize, for it meets man's most basic existential need to transcend the meaninglessness of finite existence. Not to worship One who gives you the gift of eternal life is hopelessly to misread what the gift tells you about the Giver. No more worthy candidate for deity is in principle

---

[28]For an outline of the relevant evidence in support of this contention, see Montgomery, *Christianity for the Toughminded*, p. 32. Note that in appealing to man's personal need of a conquest of death we are not falling into the error of the existentialists who claim that "truth is subjectivity": we do not base our argument for the Resurrection on man's subjective need of it or on an interior experience with Christ (the facticity of the Resurrection is established solely by the historical evidence for it); rather we argue that *given* the fact of the Resurrection, man's fundamental existential need of it goes far toward establishing its significance and the necessity of attributing it to no less than divine action.

[29]Dietl, "On Miracles," pp. 133–34.

imaginable than the One who conquers death in mankind's behalf. And it should go without saying that the Giver of such a gift has to be regarded as metaphysically positive ("God"), not negative (an archdemon) because of the positive character of His gift in relation to human need. In sum, the Resurrection does point unequivocally to the truth of Jesus' claim to Godhead, and cannot be left on the plane of an inexplicable anomaly requiring no inferential judgment.

> If someone were to acknowledge that Jesus performed all the actions attributed to him in the Gospels, but still asserted that "miracles" had not occurred since every action was explicable in terms of coincidence at the microphysical level, the implied conception of miracle would be so different from the one traditionally at issue that there would be no reason for any believer to take his objection seriously.[30]

The gospel events, if they can in fact be shown to have occurred, require an answer to Jesus' straightforward question, "But Whom do you say that I am?" (Matt. 16:15). Now, as then, only one answer will fit the facts.

And it should be noted with care that once the facticity of Christ's resurrection has been granted, all explanations for it reduce to two: Christ's own (He rose because He was God) and any and every interpretation of the event in contradiction to this explanation. Surely it is not difficult to make a choice here, for Jesus (unlike anyone else offering an explanation of the Resurrection) actually arose from the dead! His explanation has prima facie value as opposed to those in contradiction to it, presented as they are by persons who have not managed resurrections themselves. The very fact that a miracle is a nonanalogous

---

[30]Hugo Meynell, *God and the World: The Coherence of Christian Theism* (London: S.P.C.K., 1971), p. 97.

event offers an even greater reason than ordinarily to let it interpret itself, to seek its interpretation within itself. What other event or interpreter, after all, could help us understand it? But when we do go to the One who personally experienced the Resurrection, all gratuitous interpretations of the chariot-of-the-gods, creature-from-outer-space variety evaporate in the light of His own clear affirmation of His divine character, to which the sign of Jonah unequivocally points.

"MIRACLES CAN ALWAYS BE REDUCED TO NATURAL EVENTS"

What of the argument that one is never required to appeal to the miraculous as a category of interpretation—that all events, however strange, can be considered as falling within natural boundaries? We have already provided a partial answer to this objection in the immediately preceding discussion, in showing (1) that even some "coincidental" events, to say nothing of unique, nonanalogous events of overwhelming existential import (in particular Christ's resurrection), cry out for interpretation as genuine miracles, and (2) that the most satisfactory interpretation of an event such as the Resurrection will be the construction placed on it by the person who himself brings the event about, even if that construction involves the category of miracle.

To be sure, we are not advocating a metaphysical program of maximum miraculization; those events lacking the credentials of miracle must rigorously be subjected to natural explanation. We agree with Rev. Charles Kingsley who said of Newman's endorsement of the miracle story of St. Sturme and his donkey (they both fainted at "the intolerable scent" arising from the "vices and uncleansed hearts" of a band of unconverted Germans bathing in a river) that the story only proved that "St. Sturme had a nose"![31]

The question before us is really not whether it is theoretically *possible* to reduce all alleged miracles to natural events (anything is possible, it has been said, with the conceivable exception of squeezing toothpaste back into the tube!), but what one loses by forcing unique, nonanalogous events into established patterns. Any apparent gain in achieving trouble-free regularity in one's universe may be more than counterbalanced by the loss of rationality in one's interpretive technique ("coincidence" enters as a magic formula to explain all). The point can perhaps be seen best by example, and several effective illustrations have been offered by recent philosophical defenders of the epistemological meaningfulness of the miracle-idea. Holland writes:

> Suppose that a horse, which has been normally born and reared, and is now deprived of all nourishment (we could be completely certain of this)—suppose that, instead of dying, this horse goes on thriving (which again is something we could be completely certain about). A series of thorough examinations reveals no abnormality in the horse's condition: its digestive system is always found to be working and to be at every moment in more or less the state it would have been in if the horse had eaten a meal an hour or two before. This is utterly inconsistent with our whole conception of the needs and capacities of horses; and because it is an impossibility in the light of our prevailing conception, my objector, in the event of its happening, would expect us to abandon the conception—as though we had to have consistency at any price. Whereas the position I advocate is that the price is too high and it would be better to be left with the inconsistency.[32]

[31]See John Henry Newman, *Apologia pro Vita sua* (Garden City, N.Y.: Doubleday Image Books, 1956), pp. 75–77.

[32]Holland, "The Miraculous," p. 48.

Turning from this purely hypothetical example, Holland cites the wedding miracle at Cana (John 2:1–11) as another instance of an event which, if established by firsthand empirical observation, could not be reduced to a natural phenomenon without paying "too high a price" for consistency.

> A number of people could have been quite sure, could have had the fullest empirical certainty, that a vessel contained water at one moment and wine a moment later—good wine, as St. John says—without any device having been applied to it in the intervening time. Not that this last really needs to be added; for that any device should have existed *then* at least is inconceivable, even if it might just be argued to be a conceptual possibility now. I have in mind the very remote possibility of a liquid chemically indistinguishable from say mature claret being produced by means of atomic and molecular transformations. The device would have to be conceived as something enormously complicated, requiring a large supply of power. Anything less thorough-going would hardly meet the case, for those who are alleged to have drunk the wine were practiced wine-bibbers, capable of detecting at once the difference between a true wine and a concocted variety in the "British Wine, Ruby Type" category. However, that water could conceivably have been turned into wine in the first century A.D. by means of a device is ruled out of court at once by common understanding; and though the verdict is supported by scientific knowledge, common understanding has no need of this support. . . . At one moment, let us suppose, there was water and at another moment wine, in the same vessel, although nobody had emptied out the water and poured in the wine. This is something that could conceivably have been established with certainty. What is not conceivable is that it could have been done by a device. Nor is it conceivable that there could have been a natural cause of it. For this would have had to be the natural cause of the water's becoming wine.[33]

---

[33]*Ibid.*, pp. 49–50.

Boden employs the parallel illustration of a genuine healing of lepers—"not merely that a man is reported to have had an ulcerous rash which disappeared virtually overnight, but to have lost all his fingers in the gradual onset of the disease over the past years and to have had them fully restored."

Could we reasonably suggest, with all our knowledge— imperfect though it may be—of the nature of tissue-growth and cell-differentiation, and of the ravages of the leprosy bacillus within the human body, that such an "anomalous" event might one day be scientifically explained? I think not: such a suggestion would be at least as blatant an act of faith as the wildest claim ever made in the name of religion. . . . It is the biochemical *facts,* which might have been different (in particular in their temporal parameters), which exclude such a phenomenon from the class of unexplained events which we may hope to explain one day. To regard such a phenomenon as in principle scientifically explicable on the basis of general remarks about falsifiability and revolution in scientific knowledge would be as perverse as to insist that we should seriously regard the circulation of the blood as a matter of mere hypotheses, one which not only *could logically* be falsified, but which *might as a matter of fact* be falsified in the future.[34]

After a close analysis of miraculous healings, Jean Lhermitte of the French Academy of Medicine declared in a similar vein: "To suppose that all extraordinary, inexplicable, or apparently supernatural healings can be adequately explained by the chance operation of psychosomatic factors is to attempt to cross an unbridgeable chasm."[35]

---

[34]Boden "Miracles," pp. 140–41.

[35]Jean Lhermitte, *Le problème des miracles,* 2nd ed. (Paris: Gallimard, 1956), p. 120.

Speaking generally of the miraculous aspects of Jesus' ministry, philosopher Tan Tai Wei of Singapore argues:

Assume, say, that Jesus had really predicted his own death and resurrection, claimed his miraculous feats to be deliberate so as to demonstrate his 'Sonship' to the 'Father', and that we have empirical certainty that there were a few occasions at least where such exceptional phenomena occurred in strict coincidence with such demonstrations of his divinity. Now, one such occurrence, although enough to generate wonder, might be reasonably presumed after deliberation to be an accidentally coinciding natural phenomenon. Such a conclusion, though, would already seem unduly sceptical if, say, the raising of Lazarus was the only miracle of Jesus. For Jesus had confidently ordered the removal of the grave stone, prayed aloud that God should there prove his power, and then cried 'Lazarus, come forth!' And he did. And if such feats had indeed been so frequent as to be common in the life of such a person, then even if it be conceded that the exceptions, though unrepeatable or rarely repeatable, are nevertheless merely natural phenomena, the question still left unanswered is why the repeated coincidence of such rarity within the intentions and performances of this one man obtains. . . . At some point, abandoning scepticism would be more rational, because here some of our ordinary criteria (which are independent of religious considerations), governing the rational acceptability of purported coincidences as merely ordinary natural ones, would not be met.[36]

What the several thinkers we have just quoted are maintaining is that there is a point of diminishing returns when one insists on regarding all events, however empirically established as unique and nonanalogous, as ordinary

---

[36]Tan Tai Wei, "Recent Discussions on Miracles," *Sophia* [Australia], Vol. 11, No. 3 (October, 1972), p. 24. Some of the author's views in the realm of comparative religions are not satisfactory, but the general philosophical thrust of his article is most helpful.

events. Eventually one acquires so flexible and all-inclusive a notion of "coincidence" that the concept loses all significance and functions as a kind of asylum of ignorance. At such a juncture, a new kind of faith is introduced to avoid the pressing claims of religious faith, namely the blind faith (credulity would be a better word for it) that maintains, against all evidence, that a unique, nonanalogous event is somehow really a regular, ordinary event after all. But when this naturalistic faith is set against supernatural faith (and they must be so opposed, since both cannot be true), the former must rationally yield to the latter, since naturalistic faith flies in the face of the data, while supernatural faith is willing to go wherever the empirical evidence leads.

"SCIENCE REQUIRES US TO REDUCE MIRACLES TO NATURAL EVENTS"

Finally, we shall speak to a stronger statement of the objection just discussed. Here the critic does not merely claim that one *can* always regard alleged miracles as part of a "natural" context, but that the very character of the scientific operation *demands* that we do so. Alastair McKinnon well expresses this viewpoint in his philosophical defense of "the scientist's resolve to treat all events as subject to natural law":

> This does not mean that he insists that events should conform to some conception he already has. Nor does it mean that he disregards those which he has not yet been able to fit within such a conception. Rather, it means that he has resolved to view all events in this light. For him, *law* is a slogan; it is the way in which he proposes to look at the world. His acceptance of all events as expressions of natural law is the way in which he guides himself in his attempt to discover the real content of this conception. It is therefore essential that he refuse to treat any event as discrepant. This is not to say that certain scientists have not so

treated events upon convenient occasion. It is only to say that when they have done so they have ceased to be scientists.[37]

McKinnon is here describing a philosophy of science which reminds one strongly of the theological presuppositionalism of such thinkers as Herman Dooyeweerd and Cornelius Van Til: science (or theology) begins with its a priori as to the nature of things and no factual data can ultimately upset it because the presuppositional starting point becomes the criterion for the evaluation of all the data. Elsewhere I have argued that such an approach is self-defeating for theology since it goes against the inductive character of Christian faith, which must always begin with the facts purporting to constitute revelation, not with a presupposition as to their existence or as to the nature of theology.[38] Such aprioristic "invincible ignorance" leaves Christian faith with no positive means of establishing its truth-claim as superior to competing religious options that contradict it and vie for men's souls.

Scientifically, even less (if possible) can be said for this viewpoint, for the object of science is, after all, to comprehend facts of the world, not to create—much less presuppose—a system into which all facts must fit willy-nilly. To look for regularities in the behavior of data is entirely legitimate, and pragmatically to expect such regularities is the quintessence of wisdom; but to insist that all data conform to ordinary expectations and fit a non-

---

[37] Alastair McKinnon, " 'Miracle' and 'Paradox,' " *American Philosophical Quarterly*, Vol. 4, No. 4 (October, 1967), p. 314. Cf. also Richard Swinburne's statement (and refutation) of this viewpoint in his monograph, *The Concept of Miracle* (London: Macmillan, 1970), especially pp. 19–20.

[38] See, for example, Montgomery, "Once upon an A Priori," *Jerusalem and Athens: Critical Discussions on the Theology and Apologetics of Cornelius Van Til*, ed. E.R. Geehan (Philadelphia: Presbyterian and Reformed Publishing Co., 1971), pp. 380–92.

miraculous model is the antithesis of the scientific spirit. Models must arise as constructs to fit data, not serve as beds of Procrustes to force data into alien categories.

I have illustrated this truth in another context with reference to modern studies of the nature of light. Today's physicist, finding empirically that light tests out in a contradictory fashion as both undulatory and corpuscular (wave-like and particle-like), is even willing at that point of necessity to shelve his standard of rational consistency for the sake of the facts and conceptualize the unit of light as a "wave-particle" (the photon).[39] If the true scientist is willing—as he should be—to subordinate interpretation/explanation to the facts even if rational consistency suffers in the process, surely he cannot insist on forcing facts into the mold of substantive regularity! Regularity (like consistency) is properly employed up to the point where the data are no longer hospitable to its operation as an interpretive category: in the face of recalcitrant non-analogous uniqueness, regularity—not the facts—must yield.

We conclude with another, and no less striking illustration. One of the great scientific advances in the nineteenth century occurred with the development of the so-called periodic table of the elements through the efforts of Mendeleev and others. The table successfully arranged the known chemical elements by their properties, first according to atomic weights, later by atomic numbers. Its general utility was confirmed by the successful prediction that unknown elements would be found to fill in the gaps remaining in the table. The modern periodic table elegantly arranges the elements in columns according to

---

[39]Montgomery, *The Suicide of Christian Theology*, pp. 297–99. The entire essay of which this illustration forms a part ("The Theologian's Craft: A Discussion of Theory Formation and Theory Testing in Theology," pp. 267–313) is directly relevant to our present discussion.

valences (combining properties based on the hypothesized structure of the element's outer electron shell). One of the table's columns turns out to represent zero valence, or zero combining power, embracing the so-called "inert gases": helium, neon, argon, krypton, xenon, and radon. These elements offer no combining opportunities, since their outer electron rings are already complete (comprising stable electronic octets).

Early in the 1960s, however, against the force of this powerful conceptualization, inert gases were in fact combined chemically with other elements! At the Argonne National Laboratory, chemists (including representation from evangelical Wheaton College in Illinois) successfully produced xenon tetrafluoride,[40] and since that time other chemical combinations of "inert" gases have followed.[41] How was this achieved? by sophisticated atomic techniques unavailable until the 1960s? Not at all. "The tetra-fluoride, which was the first to be reported, is made by heating five parts, by volume, of fluorine with one part xenon, to 400°, followed by quenching in cold water"; the resulting compound is a "white solid at room temperature."[42]

But why, then, was this insight not arrived at a half century earlier?[43]

Since the discovery of the noble gases, at the turn of the century, the majority of chemists accepted the view that

[40]See H.H. Claassen, H. Selig, and J.G. Malm, *Journal of the American Chemical Society*, Vol. 84 (1962), p. 3593.

[41]Eg., xenon hexafluoroplatinate: Neil Barlett, *Proceedings of the Chemical Society* (1962), p. 218.

[42]Neil Bartlett, "New Compounds of Noble Gases: The Fluorides of Xenon and Radon," *American Scientist* (1963), p. 115.

[43]Xenon was isolated as early as 1898 by Sir William Ramsay and Morris William Travers.

these elements were incapable of forming normal chemical compounds. Undoubtedly the early electronic theories of valence strengthened this attitude by emphasizing the significance of the stable electronic octet. Although first ionization potentials of the heavier noble gases, xenon, 12.2 e.v., and radon, 10.8 e.v., are lower than for oxidizable elements such as chlorine, 13.0 e.v., and nitrogen, 14.1 e.v., and despite the apparent small influence of the electronic octet on the valence of the heavier elements, few serious attempts to prepare true compounds of the inert gases were made.[44]

The neatness of the periodic table—the elegance of a generalization—so mesmerized investigators that they did not attempt with any real seriousness to combine the "inert" elements. Generalized explanation and regular pattern, as represented by the periodic table, were so comfortable that the empirical investigation of factual particulars was neglected. The particular was subordinated to the general, the irregular to the regular, the fact to the theory—and truth suffered. I should like to think (though it may not be the case) that the evangelical Christian who was a member of the team responsible for the xenon tetrafluoride breakthrough was motivated, at least in part, by his conviction that the general must always yield to the particular, even as the graves of humanity had to open up in the face of the sheer nonanalogous uniqueness of Good Friday and Easter morning.

* * *

The conclusion of the whole matter is, then, that the more willing we are to allow empirical evidence of the unique and nonanalogous to stand, modifying our general conceptions of regularity accordingly, the better scientists and philosophers we become. And the more willing

---

[44]Bartlett, "New Compounds," p. 114.

we are as Christians to employ the biblical and classic miracle apologetic, the more effectively we can give a reason to our dark age of secularism for the hope that is within us. In this matter as in all others, clear thinking does not reduce the value of gospel proclamation; rather it serves as its handmaid.

3

Are You Having A
Fuddled Easter?

Novelist John Updike, in his poem "Seven Stanzas at Easter," describes the lightheadedness that seems to infect normally sane persons when they contemplate the meaning of Christ's resurrection. So "fuddled" are they by "the flowers, each soft Spring recurrent" that they arrive at views of the Resurrection that destroy its entire significance. At the risk of tethering the Bambi in us, who forever longs to gambol through the flower-strewn meadows of spring delight, let us pause a moment to consider three varieties of endemic Easter irrationality.

FUDDLEMENT NO. 1: JESUS ROSE "SPIRITUALLY"

Since the days of the old Fosdickian liberalism, the notion has gained currency that Jesus' resurrection was really not bodily but spiritual. A more sophisticated variation on this theme was Paul Tillich's. After noting that "the most primitive theory, and at the same time most beautifully expressed, is the physical one," and after regarding both it and the "spiritualistic" and "psychological" interpretations as inadequate, Tillich sets forth his own "restitution theory": "the ecstatic confirmation of the indestructible unity of the New Being and its bearer, Jesus of Nazareth."

The insuperable problem with all such "theories" that downplay the physical facticity of the Resurrection is that apart from the New Testament materials, no one can say *anything* significant about the Resurrection, and these documents *insist* on a physical resurrection. The resurrected Jesus is expressly distinguished from a ghost and eats fish with his disciples (Luke 24); Thomas is shown the nail prints in Jesus' hands and the wound in his side (John 20); etc., etc. To talk about the Resurrection, described only in the New Testament documents, in a way inconsistent with their clear description is to talk nonsense. It was to counteract such muddled notions that Updike wrote his poem:

> Make no mistake: if He rose at all it was as His body. . . .
> Let us not mock God with metaphor, analogy, sidestepping, transcendence;
> Making of the event a parable,
> a sign painted in the faded credulity of earlier ages:
> let us walk through the door.

FUDDLEMENT NO. 2: JESUS ROSE IN "SUPRAHISTORY"

As Updike has just suggested, another way of "mocking God" is by "transcendence." That is to say, one can agree that the physical resurrection of Jesus "really happened," but hold that it occurred in a transcendent realm—in *Geschichte,* not *Historie* (to use the terminology of Martin Kähler and the young Karl Barth); in "suprahistory" or "metahistory," not in the ordinary history subject to accepted canons of historical investigation.

On the surface, such an approach has much to commend it: you get your resurrection, but you don't have to prove it (and, more important, no one can disprove it!). Unfortunately, however, this achieves a Pyrrhic victory, first class. What you lose is (1) the doctrine of justification (not so incidentally "the article by which the Church stands or falls," according to the Reformers), since Christ was "raised again for our justification" (Rom. 4:25) and a resurrection outside our realm of historical need would do us no good; and (2) the genuine historicity of the event, since no criteria whatever exist for determining what is factual or unfactual in the cloud-cuckoo-land of suprahistory. There is no way of knowing that poker games on Saturday night, much less resurrections on Easter morning, occur in a transcendent sphere subject to no historical testability.

Metahistory is evasion. Rudolf Bultmann was right for once when he maintained, contrary to Barth, that if you are going to enter the sphere of *geschichtliche* resurrection, the only sensible thing to do is to engage in forthright demythologization. But, then, *pace* Bultmann, you must face the overwhelming primary-source testimony of eyewitnesses who unabashedly claim with Peter: "We have not followed cunningly devised fables [Gr. *mythoi*], when we made known unto you the power and coming of our Lord Jesus Christ, but were eyewitnesses of his majesty" (2 Pet. 1:16).

FUDDLEMENT NO. 3: JESUS ROSE IN HISTORY BUT YOU CAN'T "PROVE" IT

One might suppose that the documentary passage just cited would constitute, at least hypothetically, the kind of "proof" that is marshaled for any historical event. "No matter," the orthodox presuppositionalists and pietists inform us. "You can't 'prove' the Resurrection. It's a matter of proper starting point and faith. To deny this is to deny total depravity and the power of the Spirit."

Some years ago the Trinity Evangelical Divinity School was visited by a team of class three fuddlers from a certain Calvinist institution that shall remain nameless; they distributed their periodical, *Synapse II,* which featured an article entitled, "The Impropriety of Evidentially Arguing for the Resurrection." How sad! In former times, when minstrels traveled from hearth to hearth they brought merriment and hope.

The fuddled reasoning here is, as a matter of fact, revealed by another and better traveler—the apostle Paul. On the Areopagus he presents Christ's resurrection as the capstone of his case for the truth of the gospel (Acts 17:19–31). In 1 Corinthians 15 he blends *kerygma* with *apologia* by offering a list of eyewitness testimonies to the evidential fact of the Resurrection. In his stand before Agrippa and Festus (Acts 26), he not only assumes that these sin-blinded sinners can evidentially arrive at the facticity of the Resurrection ("Why should it be thought a thing incredible with you, that God should raise the dead?") but also appeals to a common ground of evidential knowledge ("The king knoweth of these things, before whom also I speak freely: for I am persuaded that none of these things are hidden from him; for this thing was not done in a corner").

How is it possible for Paul to do this, believing as he did in total depravity (Rom. 1–3) and in salvation through faith alone (Eph. 2:8, 9)? Simply because he recognized, as we all must, that sin did not make man nonhuman. It is one of the defining characteristics of man that he is a thinking being who, by inductive and deductive processes, evaluates the data of the world to distinguish fact from fancy.

Ironically, if man's evidential reasoning were annulled by the Fall, how would Adam have recognized God's voice subsequently calling to him in the Garden, and how would the presuppositionalist distinguish the Bible he claims to start with a priori from *Playboy* magazine?

Christian faith is not blind faith or credulity; it is grounded in fact. To talk about a real but unprovable resurrection is as foolish as to talk about suprahistorical or spiritual resurrections. They are all cop-outs—sincere, certainly, but terribly harmful in an age longing to hear the meaningful affirmation, "He is risen!"

Let's stop the fuddlement. Let's go beyond A. H. Ackley's "You ask me how I know he lives? He lives within my heart," and proclaim to a lost society that Jesus lives in our hearts because he first of all rose in the very history in which we are embedded.

4

How Muslims Do Apologetics:

The Apologetic Approach of Muhammad Ali and Its Implications for Christian Apologetics

During the early decades of the present century, Christian apologetics suffered a considerable loss of popularity and prestige. Reactionary defenders of the faith such as William Jennings Bryan (at the Scopes evolution trial in 1925) disgusted laymen and clergymen alike. The growing strength of Protestant modernism, with its tolerant attitude toward religious differences, was heralded by the publication of such works as *"Yes, But—": the Bankruptcy of Apologetics* by Willard L. Sperry, Dean of the Harvard Divinity School,[1] as well as by the various volumes of the Laymen's Foreign Missions Inquiry, which

---

[1]Issued in 1931 by Harper and Brothers, New York.

attempted to redefine the goal of missionary activity in terms of cooperative interaction among the various world religions.[2] In spite of modernism's decreasing influence following World War II, the average American still seems to accept the following philosophy:

> It doesn't . . . make too much difference whether you are Protestant, Catholic, or Jewish, or, for that matter, Hindu or Mohammedan. They are all different ways to the same goal. Basically they follow the same moral code and the religious uplift is the same. . . . Probably the religion of the future will succeed in incorporating the best insights of them all. Christian missionaries, therefore, should not impose their views on others but should rather sit at a round table and pool their views for the good of all. Confucious, Lao-tse, Asoka, Socrates, Plato, Aristotle, and then finally Jesus! These are the great leaders of mankind.[3]

Those whose thinking operates on a more logical and less emotional basis have seldom been satisfied with this kind of approach, however. The various religions of the world maintain vital beliefs that are reciprocally contradictory—tenets that are absolutely irreconcilable in many instances. To the Christian, Jesus is "Very God of Very God"; to the Jew or the Muslim, this is blasphemy. To the Christian, human sin was dealt with on the cross by substitutionary atonement; to the Eastern believer in *karma* and to the adherent of Islam such a concept is not only meaningless, but positively immoral. Obviously, such opposing views as these cannot both be right; both views may be wrong, but both cannot be correct. Since,

---

[2]*Re-thinking Missions* was published in 1932. In 1933, the Inquiry issued the *Regional Reports of the Commission of Appraisal* (3 vols.), and the *Fact-finders' Reports* (4 vols). William Ernest Hocking, professor of philosophy at Harvard, headed the Inquiry. Cf. the latter's *Living Religions and a World Faith* (1940).

[3]Martin J. Heinecken, "False Hopes and the Gospel," *Christian Social Responsibility* Vol. 1 *(Existence Today)*, ed. Harold C. Letts (Philadelphia, Muhlenberg Press, 1957), p. 131.

moreover, eternal salvation (or, at a minimum, earthly happiness) is in most religious systems made contingent upon right belief, the verification of a religion becomes a matter of no little importance. Recognition of this fact in Christian circles appears to be on the upswing again, especially in the face of Marxian attempts to discredit Christian theology. "The problems of the present have moved to a deep level which calls . . . for apologetics . . .; and there are evidences that apologists are recovering their nerve and their freedom to operate, while the self-confidence of those who turned rather to the philosophy of religion is no longer so daunting."[4]

The need for a virile Christian apologetic in our day gives good reason for our stepping outside the Christian frame of reference to observe the apologetic approach of a modern adherent of a non-Christian religion. An examination of his arguments will yield valuable information, both directly and indirectly, with regard to what constitutes a meaningful and valid religious apologetic. The non-Christian apologist chosen for study here is Muhammad Ali, of Islam's Ahmadiyya movement.

THE MAN AND HIS MOVEMENT

Maulvi, or Maulana, Muhammad Ali,[5] M.A. LL.B., has been well termed "a liberally educated, devout Moslem."[6] He was born in 1875 and died in 1951,[7] and his

---

[4]Andrew K. Rule, "Apologetics," in *Twentieth Century Encyclopedia of Religious Knowledge; an Extension of the New Schaff-Herzog*, ed. L.A. Loethscher (Grand Rapids: Baker Book House, 1955), Vol. 1, p. 53. Note the publication in 1947 of Alan Richardson's *Christian Apologetics*.

[5]No attempt will be made in this paper to utilize an official system of diacritical marks in transliterating Arabic proper names.

[6]Robert Ernest Hume, *The World's Living Religions*, rev. ed. (New York: Scribner, 1924), p. 292.

[7]See S. Muhammad Tufail's obituary for Muhammad Ali in the December, 1951, issue of the *Islamic Review*.

lifetime devotion to the Islamic cause is accurately re-
flected in a prolific literary output: *Muhammad the
Prophet; Early Caliphate; The Babi Religion; Manual of
Hadīth; New World Order; The Living Thoughts of the
Prophet Muhammad; An Urdu Commentary of the Holy
Qur'ān; An Urdu Commentary of Sahīh Bukhārī; The
Religion of Islam; The Holy Qur'ān, Containing the
Arabic Text with English Translation and Commentary.*[8]
The latter work is cited by Robert Hume as one of five
standard English translations of the entire Koran,[9] and is
listed as one of the three authoritative English translations
of the Koran in C. M. Winchell's basic *Guide to Reference
Books,* seventh edition.[10]

　　Muhammad Ali's leadership in the Lahore branch of the
Muslim Ahmadiyya movement makes it important to out-
line briefly the history and aims of that group.[11] James
Thayer Addison, sometime professor of the history of
religion and missions in the Episcopal Theological
School, Cambridge, Massachusetts, writes of the
Ahmadiyya:

> It began with the activity of Mirza Ghulam Ahmad in the
> village of Qadian, in the Punjab. In 1891 this Sunni
> Mohammedan declared himself to be . . . the coming
> Mahdi. Though condemned by the mullahs as a heretic, he
> maintained for the next seventeen years a vigorous prop-
> aganda in support of his claims. Three years after his death

---

[8]Only Muhammad Ali's most important and influential works have been included in this brief bibliography.

[9]Hume, *The World's Living Religions,* p. 292.

[10](Chicago: American Library Association, 1951), p. 144.

[11]Here it may be well to obviate confusion by distinguishing our Muhammad Ali
from the Khilafot leader Maulana Muhammad Ali (1878–1931), one of the great
leaders of Muslim India in the post-World War I era, and the founder of the
National Moslem University of Aligarh.

in 1908, his followers were estimated at nearly 50,000. In 1914, the sect split into two divisions, since known as the Qadian group and the Lahore group. . . . The Lahore party, more free in its tendencies, is despised by the Qadiani. . . . In keeping with their wider ambitions, they refer to their founder not as the Messiah but only as a reformer. Both parties are distinguished for their missionary zeal. Missions of one or of both sects are to be found not only in every province of India, but also in such areas as the Malay States, West Africa, and Palestine, where Moslems live under European control. . . . Both wings of the Ahmadiyya are busy in the production of literature and the promotion of reforms, and they offer to the young Moslem today his best chance for fellowship with a community, which, though heterodox, is thoroughly alive and in many directions progressive. The whole movement, it should be added, is markedly and often bitterly anti-Christian.[12]

Reference to the Ahmadiyya movement as "heterodox" should not lead us to believe that Muhammad Ali and other members of the Lahore society are presenting a fundamentally unique variety of Islam. The adherents of the Lahore Ahmadiyya "have tended to come steadily closer to orthodoxy."[13] Moreover, their "heterodoxy" seems to lie chiefly in their attempt to understand the Koran without the accretions of tradition, and to engage in aggressive missionary activity.[14] The Ahmadiyya movement is "the only Moslem group seriously trying to con-

---

[12]J. T. Addison, *The Christian Approach to the Moslem: a Historical Study* (New York: Columbia University Press, 1942), pp. 209–10. Cf. also Samuel Graham Wilson, *Modern Movements among Moslems* (New York: Revell, 1916), pp. 132–39; H.A. Walter, *The Ahmadiya Movement* (London: Oxford, 1918); Stanley Brush, "Ahmadiyyat in Pakistan," *The Muslim World,* April, 1955; W.C. Smith, article "Ahmadiyya,"*Encyclopaedia of Islam,* new edition.

[13]Kenneth Cragg, *The Call of the Minaret* (New York: Oxford University Press, 1956), p. 249.

[14]*Ibid.*, p. 250.

vert Western Christians'';[15] that this should produce
inter-Muslim conflict is understandable when one recalls
the historic apathy of Islam to nonviolent propagation of
the faith. Consider, for example, the following statements
in Douglas C. McMurtrie's widely used history of printing:

> Islam, in marked contrast to Buddhism, was uncompromis-
> ingly opposed to the reduplication of its sacred writings
> through the medium of print. The reason for this opposition
> is not clear, but in all probability it was simply religious
> conservatism. The Koran had been given to the Moslems in
> written form, and writing, therefore, was the only means by
> which it might ever be transmitted. To this day the Koran
> has never been printed from type in any Mohammedan
> country; is it always reproduced by lithography.[16]

THE CONTENT OF MUHAMMAD ALI'S APOLOGETIC

Having obtained an overview of Muhammad Ali and the
movement with which he has been identified, let us
examine in detail his defense of Islam. Muhammad Ali's

---

[15] Addison, *The Christian Approach to the Moslem*, p. 209. An exception may be
made to groups working among blacks in the United States. Consult: C. Umhau
Wolf, "Muslims in the American Mid-West," *The Muslim World* (Jan., 1960);
C. Braden, "Islam in America," *International Review of Missions* (July, 1959);
C. Braden, "Moslem Missions in America," *Religion in Life* (summer, 1959);
N. Makdisi, "The Moslems of America," *The Christian Century* (August 26,
1959).

[16] Douglas C. McMurtrie, *The Book; the Story of Printing and Bookmaking*, 3rd
rev. ed. (London and New York: Oxford University Press, 1943), p. 93. The
strictly orthodox Muslim Marmaduke Pickthall is careful not to title his English
translation of the Koran simply *The Koran*, or *The Glorious Koran*, but rather
The Meaning of the Glorious Koran (New York: Knopf, 1930). He states in his
Foreword, "The Koran cannot be translated. That is the belief of old-fashioned
Sheykhs and the view of the present writer." [Yet A.A. Paton, in his *A History
of the Egyptian Revolution* (London: Trubner, 1870, second ed. enlarged, Vol.
2. p. 245) wrote: "The printing of the Koran has always been resisted by the
Ulema as unlawful; but, for the first time in the history of Islamism, an edition of
the Koran was set up in type, and the Mufti of Cairo, Sheikh-el-Temimy, was
asked to set his seal of permission upon it in order to ensure its sale"—Ed. of
The Muslim World.]

two main writings will be utilized in this connection: his edition and translation of the Koran,[17] and his systematic presentation of *The Religion of Islam*.[18] One who studies these two volumes discovers that the author's apologetic for Islam has a negative and a positive side. Negatively, Islam's chief rival, Christianity, is criticized; positively, the claim is made that Islam harmonizes with the modern scientific and philosophical *Weltanschauung,* possesses a divinely inspired scripture, and is experientially self-attesting. Each of these apologetic arguments will now be set forth.

Christianity: a false religion

Samuel M. Zwemer, late missionary to those of the Islamic faith, well characterized the general Ahmadiyya attitude toward Christianity when he wrote:

The old Islam honoured Jesus Christ as a great prophet, and although it denied his deity and atoning death it always acknowledged his sinlessness and virgin birth. The New Islam denies the sinlessness of Jesus, mocks at the virgin birth, and offers proof from the writings of infidels and from modern destructive criticism that the Bible is a tissue of fables and myths. It is painful to read the articles written on these subjects by men who in some cases are graduates of Christian colleges.[19]

---

[17]This work has gone through three editions containing Arabic text and English translation (1st ed., Woking, England, *Islamic Review,* 1917; 2nd ed., Lahore, Ahmadiyya Anjuman-i-Ishatt-i-Islam, and Woking and London, Unwin, 1920; 3d ed., Lahore, Almadiyya Anjuman-i-Ishatt-i-Islam, 1935); and two editions without the Arabic text and with abridged notes have been published (in 1928 and 1934). References of this paper will in all cases be to the unabridged 3rd ed., a copy of which I obtained from Lahore, together with Muhammad Ali's *Religion of Islam.*

[18]I shall refer to the latest edition: *The Religion of Islam: a Comprehensive Discussion of the Sources, Principles and Practices of Islam,* 2nd ed. (Lahore, Ahmadiyyah Anjuman Ishaat Islam, 1950 2nd ed. first pub. in 1935).

[19]Samuel M. Zwemer, *Across the World of Islam: Studies in Aspects of the Mohammedan Faith and in the Present Awakening of the Moslem Multitudes* (New York: Revell, 1929), p. 28.

Both Ahmadiyya groups have rejected the traditional belief (orthodox but not koranic) "which had come into Islam after its expansion, relating to Christ as returning from Heaven to the world in order to subdue anti-Christ and bring in a Muslim millennial state of bliss and righteousness."[20] Although Muhammad Ali is by no means as crass in his criticisms of Christianity as some Ahmadiyya writers,[21] his position is nevertheless strongly negative toward the New Testament and toward Christian views of Christ. Muhammad Ali maintains that Jesus was sinless, for he was a prophet and all prophets are without sin; but in his moral purity Jesus did not differ at all from Adam or Moses or John the Baptist, who were also prophets (*Holy Qur'ān*, pp. 159–62, 612, 615; *Religion of Isam*, pp. 232–40). Christian theology has made a grievous error in asserting that Jesus is the unique Son of God (*Holy Qur'ān*, pp. 272–74). The resurrection and ascension of Jesus never took place (he did not actually die as a result of crucifixion, but much later suffered a natural death); the Second Coming of Christ is an unwarranted hope (*Holy Qur'ān*, pp. 241–44; *Religion of Islam*, p. 262). "Recent criticism has shown that the Christians have only followed previous idolatrous nations in deifying a man" (*Holy Qur'ān*, p. 274). He claims that the Christian church has been led to these false beliefs by strict reliance upon the Bible as historically accurate. However, "modern criticism of the Bible, together with the accessibility of ancient manuscripts, has now established the fact that many alterations were made in it. . . . Even the Gospels are admitted to have been altered. The original Gospel of Jesus

---

[20]Cragg, *The Call of the Minaret*, p. 250.

[21]E.g. those who have written for the periodical, *Review of Religions*. See Canon H.U. Weitbrecht, "Reform Movements in India," ch. 19 of *Islam and Missions*, ed. Wheery, Zwemer, and Mylrea (New York: Revell, 1911) p. 281; and Zwemer, *Across the World of Islam*, p. 29.

Christ is nowhere to be found. . . . Many . . . examples of changes made in the text can be quoted. . . . Commenting on . . . Mk. 10:17, Dummelow [*The One Bible Commentary* (London, Macmillan, 1913] says . . .: 'The author of Matthew . . . altered the text slightly, to prevent the reader from supposing that Christ denied that He was good' " (*Religion of Islam,* pp. 212–14).

Islam: philosophically and scientifically sound

In Muhammad Ali's opinion, Islam, more than any other religion, accords with the dynamic, evolutionary world-view of twentieth-century science and philosophy. He writes:

> With the advent of Islam, religion has received new significance. Firstly, it is to be treated not as a dogma, which a man must accept if he will escape everlasting damnation, but as a science based on the universal experience of humanity. It is not this or that nation that becomes the favourite of God and the recipient of Divine revelation; on the contrary, revelation is recognized as a necessary factor in the evolution of man. Hence while in its crudest form it is the universal experience of humanity, in its highest, that of prophetical revelation, it has been a Divine gift bestowed upon all nations of the world. And the idea of the scientific in religion has been further strengthened by presenting its doctrines as principles of action. There is not a single doctrine of religion which is not made the basis of action for the development of man to higher and yet higher stages of life. Secondly, the sphere of religion is not confined to the next world; its primary concern is rather with this life, and that man, through a righteous life here on earth, may attain to the consciousness of a higher existence (*Religion of Islam,* pp. 5–6).

The Koran: divinely inspired

Muhammad Ali is at pains to demonstrate that the Koran, in its origin, transmission, arrangement, and lofty subject matter, is indeed the final revelation of God to men (*Holy Qur'ān*, Preface, pp. xxviii–xcii; *Religion of Islam*, pp. 17–57). It is asserted that the Koran contains no discrepancies; the theory of abrogation (not entirely dissimilar to the Christian notion of "progressive revelation") is rejected (*Religion of Islam*, pp. 35–44; *Holy Qur'ān*, pp. lxxv–xcii).

Muhammad Ali's translation of the Koran tries, within the limits of Arabic vocabulary and syntax, to tone down difficult passages and thus to provide the twentieth-century reader with a more scientifically and historically palatable text. For example, Muhammad Ali removes any notion of miracles from the statement of Joseph in Egypt to his brothers as given in Surah 12:93. George Sale's translation has, "Depart ye with this my inner garment, and throw it on my father's face; and he shall recover his sight."[22] J. M. Rodwell translates the same verse: "Go ye with this my shirt and throw it on my father's face, and he shall recover his sight."[23] Marmaduke Pickthall expresses it thus: "Go with this shirt of mine and lay it on my father's face, he will become (again) a seer."[24] However, Muhammad Ali renders the verse, "Take this my shirt and cast it before my father, he will come to know" (*Holy Qur'ān*, p. 493). Professor Arthur Jeffery is unjust in citing this as evidence that Muhammad Ali's translation is "doctored" and "forced" (because Muhammad Ali goes against the traditional understanding of the passage);[25] the

---

[22]*The Koran*, trans. George Sale; 8th ed. (Philadelphia: Lippincott, 1878), p. 198 (second numeration).

[23]*The Koran*, trans. J.M. Rodwell (London: Dent; New York: Dutton [Everyman's Library, no. 380], 1909), p. 238.

[24]Pickthall, *The Meaning of the Glorious Koran*, p. 246.

[25]Arthur Jeffery, "New Trends in Moslem Apologetic," ch. 20 of *The Moslem World of To-day*, ed. John R. Mott (New York: Dotan, 1925), pp. 318–19. Comments of the Baidawi and Jallalo'ddin on the passage in question are given in Sale's translation of *The Koran*.

Arabic word *'basīr'* can mean either "one who sees things with the eyes" or "one endowed with mental perception, one knowing," as Pickthall's mediating translation indicates. But we do have in Muhammad Ali's version an obvious apologetic attempt to make the Koran relevant to the modern mind. The fulfillment of koranic prophecy is cited by Muhammad Ali as a further proof of the Koran's divine origin. Particular emphasis is placed upon the prophecy of Islam's triumph.

> The Holy Qur'ān gives prominence to the great prophecy of the triumph of Islam, and its earlier chapters are full of such prophecies uttered in various forms. Now these chapters were revealed, and these prophecies announced, at a time when the Holy Prophet was quite alone and helpless, beset by enemies on all sides plotting to put an end to his very life. . . . Yet under these circumstances, amid all this despair on every side, we find prophecy after prophecy announced in the surest and most certain terms to the effect that the great forces of opposition should be brought to naught, that the enemies of Islam should be put to shame and perish, that Islam should become the religion of the whole of Arabia, that the empire of Islam should be established and battles be fought in which the Muslims should be victorious and the enemy brought low, that Islam should spread to the farthest corners of the earth and that it should ultimately be triumphant over all religions of the world. . . . Was not all this brought to fulfillment, against all expectations, in the lifetime of the Holy Prophet? (*Religion of Islam*, pp. 248–50).

Islam: experientially verifiable

Muhammad Ali makes every effort to stress the simplicity of, and the pragmatic values inherent in, the Muslim faith.[26]

---

[26]Cragg, *The Call of the Minaret*, pp. 252–306.

The Islamic beliefs are really axiomatic truths upon which
are based the moral and spiritual aspects of the life of
man. . . . The precepts of Islam which inculcate duties
towards God and duties towards man are based on that
deep knowledge of human nature which cannot be possessed but by the Author of that nature. They cover the
whole range of the different grades of the development of
man, and are thus wonderfully adapted to the requirements
of different peoples. In the Holy Qur'ān are found guiding
rules for the ordinary man of the world as well as for the
philosopher, and for communities in the lowest grade of
civilization as well as for the highly civilized nations of the
world. Practicability is the keynote of its precepts, and thus
the same universality which marks its principles of faith is
to be met with in its practical ordinances, suiting as they do
the requirements of all ages and nations" (Holy Qur'ān, p.
xiii).

A CRITIQUE OF MUHAMMAD ALI'S APOLOGETIC AND ITS BEARING UPON THE CHRISTIAN *DEFENSIO FIDEI*

Muhammad Ali Criticized

Arguments in support of a religious viewpoint normally
fall into one of two general categories, the rational or the
empirical. A rational apologetic attempts to show that the
religious belief is philosophically sound and conforms to
the best dictates of reason, while an empirical apologetic
tries to prove that the religion harmonizes with factual
experience. Empirical arguments can be objective or subjective in nature, depending upon whether harmony with
external experience (history, physical and natural science) or conformity with internal (psychological) experience is stressed.[27] The following table summarizes the
most common apologetic arguments used to support reli-

---

[27]Strictly speaking, all apologetic arguments are rational in type, for Kant has
shown that philosophical presuppositions precede all forms of empirical in-

gious conceptions and classifies these arguments according to their rational or empirical character.

Rational Defenses	Empirical Defenses	
	Objective	Subjective
1. The religion is deducible from self-evident a prioris.	1. The scriptures (or doctrines) of the religion fit the historical and scientific facts of experience.	1. The religion is pragmatically sound.
2. The religion conforms to the philosophical viewpoint or presuppositions generally accepted (the philosophical *Zeitgeist*).	2. The religion has given rise to valid prophecies of future events.	2. The religion is personally meaningful and self-validating in the life of the believer.
3. The scriptures (or doctrines) of the religion are internally self-consistent.	3. The religion has given rise to valid miraculous happenings.	3. The religion gives rise to answered prayer. (May be an objectively empirical argument).

Muhammad Ali's attempt at refuting Christianity does not fit into the table of apologetic arguments at any point. The reason for this is simply that such refutations are not "apologies" or defenses at all, but are *ad hominem* arguments of an offensive nature. Even if one were to grant that Muhammad Ali had disproven Christianity, this would not add a grain of evidence in support of Islam, for Islam (and all other religions, for that matter) could still be false. The falsity of one religion, in other words, is not

---

quiry. However, the a prioris of empirical investigation (to be distinguished sharply from those of logical positivism) are of a simple, self-evident variety, and instead of precluding discovery and intellectual progress, seem to provide valuable tools for investigative activity. Therefore, it appears wise to retain the distinction between rational and empirical arguments—a distinction incidentally, which is fundamental in understanding the role and development of modern science.

proof of the truth of another. Unfortunately, the Ahmadiyya movements have been almost totally blind to this fact in their propaganda activities.

Strictly speaking, Muhammad Ali does not try to show that Islam is deducible from self-evident a prioris, for he recognizes that the Muslim faith is based on historical revelation. However, as we have seen, he does claim that Islam conforms to the activistic, evolutionary *Weltanschauung* of modern scientific and cultural philosophy. Unlike the medieval Averroës, who, in his treatise, *The Agreement of Religion and Philosophy*, asserted that the Aristotelian philosophy of his time could not be reconciled with koranic teaching,[28] Muhammad Ali affirms that contemporary secular thought and Islamic doctrine blend perfectly. The fallacy in such an argument lies in the fact that the philosophical scene is kaleidoscopic—that the *Zeitgeist* is never an absolute. The static universe of one era became the relativistic, evolutionary universe of the next; and who is to say what cosmological views future generations will hold? Conformity to current philosophical views (even if granted) is therefore no proof of the validity of a religion. A second rational argument presented by Muhammad Ali is his claim that the Koran is internally consistent—that it contains no internal contradictions. This apologetic is likewise of little consequence, for the self-consistency of a writing does not prove that it is divine revelation. Euclid's Geometry, for example, is not self-contradictory at any point, but no one claims that this work is therefore divinely inspired in some unique sense.

When we consider Muhammad Ali's objectively empir-

---

[28]See Etienne Gilson, *Reason and Revelation of the Middle Ages* (New York: Scribner, 1938), ch. 2.

ical defenses of Muslim faith, we find that he employs the
first two arguments given in the table above, but not the
third one. Miracles, he believes, are next to impossible to
prove, and therefore of little attesting value;[29] moreover,
"the Holy Qur'ān makes it clear that the bringing about of
a transformation is the real object for which prophets are
raised up, that this object is attained by several means,
each of which, therefore, has but a secondary value, and
that among these evidences of the truth of the Prophet the
miracle occupies not the highest place" (*Religion of Islam,* p. 243). For Muhammad Ali, "the greatest miracle of
Islam is the Holy Qur'ān (*ibid,.* p. 244), and therefore he is
concerned, as we have seen, to show that the Koran is
scientifically and historically sound and contains true
prophecies. To demonstrate that a writing is accurate in
its historic and scientific statements, however, no more
proves that it is divinely inspired than when one shows
that the volume is internally consistent. Numerous accurate scientific and historical treatises have been written
which lay no claim to divine inspiration, and for which no
such claim has been made by their readers.

With regard to the evidential value of prophecy, one is
on more solid ground, if fulfilled prophecy of sufficient
worth can be cited. But the qualification just stated poses
a real problem, for many prophecies of the Delphic oracle
variety have been made through history. Moreover, the
koranic prophecy of Islam's ultimate triumph is of little
significance, for though Islam experienced a very rapid

---

[29]"There is one great disadvantage attaching to all miracles which are merely
manifestations of power. It is very difficult to secure reliable evidence for them
under all circumstances. . . . Another difficulty in the matter of miracle generally is to be found in the fact that however wonderful a performance, it may be
explained scientifically, and thus lose all value as a sign of the Divine mission of
its workers" (*Religion of Islam,* p. 246).

early spread, the later history of the religion has been anything but triumphant.[30] In 1924, in fact, a member of the Ahmadiyya movement stated in London: "We, the present-day Moslems, have indeed fallen on evil days. Our past glory has forsaken us. Our might, our honour, have deserted us."[31]

Muhammad Ali's main apologetic thrust is in the area of subjectively empirical argument. "The supreme object before the Prophet is to effect a moral and spiritual transformation; the means adopted are an appeal to the reasoning faculty, an appeal to the heart of man to convince him that the Divine message is meant for his own uplift, and lessons drawn from previous history showing how the acceptance of truth has always benefited man, and its rejection has worked to his own undoing" (*Religion of Islam*, p. 243). The difficulty with pragmatic arguments for a religion is that truths do not always work, and beliefs that work are by no means always true. Job's religious beliefs, though presumably true, did not give him uninterrupted peace of mind; and many besides Faust have discovered that the father of lies makes an effective business partner. Subjective attestation for a religion has the engaging advantage of becoming meaningful only if the individual actually attempts to believe in the religion, and then, of course, no further apologetic is necessary. But the intelligent person, faced with several religious options, needs objective, external ground for trying a religion, and he is morally within his rights to refuse to be-

---

[30]See, for example, the chapters on "Why the Spread of Islam Was Stayed" and "Low Position of Islam in the Scale of Civilization" in *Two Old Faiths*, by J.M. Mitchell and William Muir (New York, Chautauqua Press, 1891), pp. 125–52; and the section on "The Islamic Empire and Its Dissolution" in Carl Brockelmann's *History of the Islamic Peoples*, trans. Carmichael and Perlmann (New York: Putnam, 1947), pp. 107 ff.

[31]Quoted in Zwemer, *Across the World of Islam*, pp. 15–16.

come emotionally involved in a religion without good reasons to do so. Such "good reason" must of course lie in a realm other than the subjectively empirical, if a neat case of circular reasoning is to be avoided.

LESSONS FOR CHRISTIAN APOLOGISTS

The reader has undoubtedly been impressed (as has the writer) with the similarity between many of Muhammad Ali's arguments for Islam and the defenses for the Christian faith presented by not a few Christian theologians. It is safe to say that the type of theologian of whom I speak would have been only too quick to agree with the criticisms of Muhammad Ali set forth above. One wonders, however, if the great truth would have dawned that a fallacious argument is fallacious regardless of who employs it and regardless of the context in which it is used.

Specifically, no religion is deducible from self-evident a prioris, or all men in their right minds would hold the same faith.[32] Conformity to the philosophical *Zeitgeist* is no evidence for the truth of a religion, regardless of what religion it is. Internal consistency and external fitting of the facts do not prove a sacred book to be God's revelation—even if that book be the Bible. The reasonableness of religious doctrines does not prove them true (for God is presumably above reason, since he is the Author of logic), nor does it prove them false (*credo quia absurdum* is a ridiculous formula, even if reiterated by a modern philosopher of Søren Kierkegaard's stature). Pragmatic arguments for a religion are weak and posi-

---

[32]Only deductive logic and theoretical mathematics, among human disciplines, are deduced from self-evident presuppositions, and these areas, it should be carefully observed, deal with no matters-of-fact at all, but only with conceptual relationships. Even Thomas Aquinas rejected the ontological proof of God's existence.

tively misleading—even if Norman Vincent Peale asserts
them again in behalf of Christianity. The appeal to "try
such-and-such religion and you will find it self-
authenticating in your heart of hearts" is the mark of
apologetic debility, for such claims can be made by everyone from Muhammad Ali to Father Divine without fear of
refutation (there being no possible refutation for individual experience).

It is time that Christian apologists came to realize that a
string of individually weak arguments for the gospel does
not comprise one strong argument for it. Objective empirical evidence for Jesus Christ and his message is the only
truly valid Christian apologetic possible, for it alone is
subject to the canons of evidence employed in other fields
of endeavor. And what objectively empirical ground for
accepting the Christian gospel is there? Muhammad Ali
himself states it when he writes, "If Jesus did not rise from
the dead, the pillar on which the whole structure of Christianity rests crashes to the ground" (*Religion of Islam*,
p. 241). The *kerygma* of the early church, as seen in the
preaching recorded in the Book of Acts, centers its case
squarely and decisively upon the fact of Christ's resurrection, and the apostle Paul states the Christian apologetic in
no less definite terms when he writes to the Corinthians
(1 Cor. 15:1–9, 14):

> Now I would remind you, brethren, in what terms I
> preached to you the gospel, which you received, in which
> you stand, by which you are saved, if you hold it fast—
> unless you believed in vain. For I delivered to you as of first
> importance what I also received, that Christ died for our
> sins in accordance with the scriptures, that he was buried,
> that he was raised on the third day in accordance with the
> scriptures, and that he appeared to more than five hundred
> brethren at one time, most of whom are still alive, though
> some have fallen asleep. Then he appeared to James, then

to all the apostles. Last of all, as to one untimely born, he appeared also to me. For I am the least of the apostles, unfit to be called an apostle, because I persecuted the church of God. . . . If Christ has not been raised, then our preaching is in vain and your faith is in vain (1 Cor. 15:1–4, 6–9, 14).

If the Christian church is indeed on the verge of a revival of apologetic interest, it is hoped that the resurrection of Christ will be made the pivot of that interest so that the errors of Muhammad Ali will not be further duplicated in a Christian framework.[33]

---

[33]For an example of a Resurrection-centered modern work on Christian apologetics, see Wilbur M. Smith, *The Supernaturalness of Christ* (Boston: W.A. Wilde, 1940).

5

Dr. Johnson as Apologist

"Dr. Samuel Johnson's character, religious, moral, political, and literary, nay his figure and manner, are, I believe, more generally known than those of almost any man," wrote James Boswell, his inimitable biographer. Since his own day—the eighteenth-century England of the Wesleys—his portly frame, brilliant conversation, and acidic wit have rarely been forgotten. Even those entirely unaware of Johnson's immortal contributions to English lexicography recall his chauvinistic definition of oats: "a grain which in England is generally given to horses, but in Scotland supports the people." But the Yale editions of the works of Johnson and of the private papers of Boswell are currently producing a new flurry of Johnson studies and a correspondingly greater depth of interest in the intimacies of his life and world-view.

One of the consequences of the Johnson revival has been a growing awareness of the importance of religion to him. The deism and shallow skepticism of his age (the misdesignated "Enlightenment"), Boswell's loose morals, and Johnson's crusty, nonpietistic life-style have doubtless contributed to the general impression that religion played a very small part in his life. Recent studies, however, have shown that such an impression could not be further from the truth. Whether one reads Maurice Quinlan's *Samuel Johnson: A Layman's Religion* (1964)—the first book-length study of the subject in the twentieth century—or Chester Chapin's *The Religious Thought of Samuel Johnson* (1968), or English biographer Peter Quennell's recent *Samuel Johnson: His Friends and Enemies,* the same portrait emerges. In Quennell's words: "Johnson was a Christian Fundamentalist, who admitted no compromise, but asserted the unshakable truth of every major point of Christian doctrine."

That this is no exaggeration can be seen both from the intimate details of his spiritual life and from his numerous conversational declarations on religion. As a student at Oxford, he was deeply touched by William Law's *Serious Call to a Holy Life;* Johnson himself would later compose an informal diary of prayers (published only posthumously). These *Prayers and Meditations* show us that Johnson placed all aspects of his existence *sub specie aeternitatis.* On beginning the second volume of his *Dictionary,* he prayed, for example: "O God, Who hast hitherto supported me, enable me to proceed in this labour, and in the whole task of my present state; that when I shall render up at the last day in account of the talent committed to me, I may receive pardon for the sake of Jesus Christ." When he began *The Rambler* he prayed: "Grant, I beseech Thee, that in this my undertaking, Thy Holy Spirit may not be withheld from me, but that I may promote Thy glory, and the salvation both of myself and others."

Though temperamentally aligned with seventeenth-century orthodoxy rather than eighteenth-century pietism, Johnson had a "wonderful" religious experience in February, 1784, during the last year of his life; this experience was what we would today term an entry into the "deeper life" or perhaps even a "second blessing," and Chapin comments on it that "in the last months of his life Johnson adopted a view of conversion not unlike that held by many Evangelicals."

Conversationally, Johnson's thoroughgoing Christian orthodoxy was so plain and forthright that it was a constant embarrassment to mediating friends who had absorbed the eighteenth-century *Zeitgeist*.

"What do you mean by damned?" the amiable Dr. Adams once asked him. Johnson answered (passionately and loudly), "Sent to Hell, Sir, and punished everlastingly."

Mrs. Adams replied, "You seem, Sir, to forget the merits of our Redeemer."

Johnson said, "Madam, I do not forget the merits of my Redeemer; but my Redeemer has said that He will set some on His right hand and some on His left."

Johnson had absolutely no patience with the deists or skeptics of his day. He unmercifully criticized Boswell for having visited Rousseau: "Rousseau, Sir, is a very bad man. I would sooner sign a sentence for his transportation, than that of any felon who has gone from the Old Bailey these many years. Yes, I should like to have him work in the plantations." Boswell asked, "Sir, do you think him as bad a man as Voltaire?" Johnson replied "Why, Sir, it is difficult to settle the proportions of iniquity between them."

But Johnson not only affirmed an uncompromising biblical orthodoxy; he vigorously defended it in an age when such thinkers as David Hume were eroding confidence in the veracity of Christian faith. Here are typical examples of Johnson's apologetic method:

> It is always easy to be on the negative side. If a man were now to deny that there is salt upon the table, you could not

reduce him to an absurdity. Come, let us try this a little further. I deny that Canada is taken, and I can support my denial by pretty good arguments. The French are a much more numerous people than we, and it is not likely that they would allow us to take it. "But the ministry have assured us, in all the formality of the Gazette, that it is taken."— Very true. But the ministry have put us to an enormous expense by the war in America, and it is their interest to persuade us that we have got something for our money.— "But the fact is confirmed by thousands of men who were at the taking of it."—Ay, but these men have still more interest in deceiving us. They don't want that you should think the French have beat them, but that they have beat the French. Now suppose you should go over and find that it is really taken, that would only satisfy yourself; for when you come home we will not believe you. We will say, you have been bribed. Yet, Sir, notwithstanding all these plausible objections, we have no doubt that Canada is really ours. Such is the weight of common testimony. How much stronger are the evidences of the Christian religion?

For revealed religion (Johnson said), there was such historical evidence, as, upon any subject not religious, would have left no doubt. Had the facts recorded in the New Testament been mere civil occurrences, no one would have called in question the testimony by which they are established; but the importance annexed to them, amounting to nothing less than the salvation of mankind, *raised a cloud* in their minds, and created doubts unknown upon any other subject. Of proofs to be derived from history, one of the most cogent, he seemed to think, was the opinion so well authenticated, and so long entertained, of a Deliverer that was to appear about that time. . . . For the immediate life and miracles of Christ, such attestation as that of the apostles, who all, except St. John, confirmed their testimony with their blood; such belief as their witness procured from a people best furnished with the means of judging, and least disposed to judge favourably; such an extension afterwards of that belief over all the nations of the earth, though originating from a nation of all others most despised, would leave no doubt that the things witnessed were true, and were of a nature more than human.

With respect to evidence, Dr. Johnson observed that we had not such evidence that Caesar died in the Capitol, as that Christ died in the manner related.

Chapin correctly observes that "bypassing the traditional theistic proofs, Johnson chose to discuss revealed religion only. . . . Johnson's own method of 'establishing' revelation is the common-sense one of attempting to show that the events narrated in the Bible—at least those important to Christians—are solidly grounded in fact. It is clear that *all* arguments in favor of theism, or 'natural religion,' as the eighteenth century called it, seemed to Johnson less important than those which tended to establish revelation itself as solidly grounded in the facts of history."

Blessed Johnson! He avoided the twin shoals of scholastic Thomism (thereby giving no ammunition to the deists) and of pietistic presuppositionalism (thereby not leaving Christianity without a witness). When I visited Johnson's Gough Square house in London—the very house where he prayed his prayers on commencing the *Dictionary* and *The Rambler*—I myself had a "wonderful" experience, and I prayed that his like might arise and flourish for Christ's sake in our day.

6

Once Upon an A Priori

VAN TIL IN LIGHT OF THREE FABLES

Much learned controversy has accompanied Cornelius Van Til's apologetic endeavors throughout his long and productive career. The *rabies theologorum* has raged between Van Til and other Calvinists as to whose apologetic methodology is *truly* Reformed. Large portions of Van Til's writings attempt to distinguish his "genuinely Protestant" approach from what he regards as weakened and compromising variants of Reformed theology ("evangelicalism" or "Arminianism"—a general category in which the fundamentalist *Schwärmer* finds himself in the same bed with Anglican lay apologist C. S. Lewis and Lutheran dogmatician Francis Pieper).

Though by no means a stranger to controversy myself, I do not wish to increase the height of what appears to be a dangerously top-heavy pile or refutations and counter-refutations. At the same time, I am too concerned about the non-Christian's plight in the contemporary world of growing secularity to by-pass the question of apologetic

107

method so ably raised by Van Til. Perhaps a way to discuss the latter without contributing directly to the deadly in-fighting among apologists for historic Christian verities is to proceed in a parabolic manner. Let it be noted, however, that the use of parables here is strictly literary; it must not be construed as a presuppositional, prior commitment to parabolic technique as biblically revealed!

The Universe of Tlön

All is yellow to the jaundiced eye. As he speaks of the facts the sinner reports them to himself and others as yellow every one. There are no exceptions to this. And it is the facts as reported to himself, that is as distorted by his own subjective condition, which he assumes to be the facts as they really are.[1]

What then more particularly do I mean by saying that epistemologically the believer and the non-believer have nothing in common? I mean that every sinner looks through colored glasses. And these colored glasses are cemented to his face. He assumes that self-consciousness is intelligible without God-consciousness. He assumes that consciousness of facts is intelligible without consciousness of God.[2]

Shall we in the interest of a point of contact admit that man can interpret anything correctly if he virtually leaves God out of the picture? Shall we who wish to prove that nothing can be explained without God, first admit that some things at least can be explained without him? On the contrary we shall show that all explanations without God are futile.[3]

[1]Cornelius Van Til, "Introduction" to *The Inspiration and Authority of the Bible* by B.B. Warfield (Philadelphia: Presbyterian and Reformed Publishing Co., 1948), p. 20.

[2]Van Til, *A Christian Theory of Knowledge* (Philadelphia: Presbyterian and Reformed Publishing Co., 1969), p. 295.

[3]*Ibid.*, p. 294.

These statements set forth both Van Til's analysis of the human condition and his apologetic program with its powerful appeal to Christian believers who "know" in their heart of hearts that Christianity is true, that the Bible is God's Word, and that by the work of the Holy Spirit *their* colored glasses have been de-cemented from their faces (or at least rendered sufficiently transparent for them to know the Truth), while non-Christians remain imprisoned in a jaundiced view of total reality. But now (in a disquietingly unbelieving manner—which is both legitimate and necessary in apologetic discussion, since apologetics by definition always directs itself to *unbelievers*), let us consider a reversal of Van Til's approach. Let us contemplate the hypothetical situation in which the Christian is treated as an unbeliever in an exactly parallel fashion by the onslaught of an antithetical ideology (antichristic, but claiming to be christic, as all such viewpoints do).

The blind Argentinian bibliophile and littérateur Jorge Luis Borges sets out just this situation in his profound short story, "Tlön, Uqbar, Orbis Tertius." A secret society of hermetic, cabalistic, and rosicrucian bent conceives of the idea of producing a total philosophy of life in the form of a detailed and full description of the world as it "really" is. The society's work in creating the new world comes to the attention of an ascetic and nihilistic American millionaire:

At that time the twenty volumes of the *Encyclopaedia Britannica* were circulating in the United States; Buckley suggested that a methodical encyclopedia of the imaginary planet be written. He was to leave them his mountains of gold, his navigable rivers, his pasture lands roamed by cattle and buffalo, his Negroes, his brothels and his dollars, on one condition: "The work will make no pact with the impostor Jesus Christ." Buckley did not believe in God, but he wanted to demonstrate to this nonexistent God that mortal man was capable of conceiving a world.[4]

Subsequently, the *First Encyclopaedia of Tlön* was allowed to reach the public. It employed the strategy of "exhibiting a world which is not too incompatible with the real world," and thus served to prepare the way for a future *Second Encyclopaedia,* written in one of the languages of the imaginary world and so fully and effectively reinterpreting the traditional picture of the universe that "the world will be Tlön."[5] The success of the total plan was assured by the response to the *First Encyclopaedia* in our own time:

> Manuals, anthologies, summaries, literal versions, authorized re-editions and pirated editions of the Greatest Work of Man flooded and still flood the earth. Almost immediately, reality yielded on more than one account. The truth is that it longed to yield. Ten years ago any symmetry with a semblance of order—dialectical materialism, anti-Semitism, Nazism—was sufficient to entrance the minds of men. How could one do other than submit to Tlön, to the minute and vast evidence of an orderly planet?[6]

Borges' point is simply that men have a weakness for "orderly" views of the universe and have been quite willing, again and again, to commit themselves to horrifying philosophies of life for the sake of ordering their experience. Now Van Til would readily agree with this. He would go even farther than Borges: the non-Christian inevitably creates Tlöns because of his jaundiced, sin-

---

[4]Jorge Luis Borges, *Labyrinths: Selected Stories & Other Writings,* ed. Donald A. Yates and James E. Irby (New York: New Directions, 1964), p. 15.

[5]*Ibid.,* p. 18.

[6]*Ibid.,* p. 17.

impregnated condition. The "facts" of the world, though contrary to such myth-making, are powerless to stop it, since the unbeliever will twist them as he will, in the interests of his unbelief.

But consider: *if* "there are no exceptions" to the jaundiced vision of the sinner, and sin is a universal condition to which both non-Christian and Christian are subject (as all holding to Romans 3:23 must admit), then *how* is Tlön to be distinguished from reality? Which is the devil's city and which the *civitas Dei?* From Van Til's viewpoint, the internal consistency of the world-picture cannot serve as a naked test, for Tlön will be regarded as consistent by the sinners who propose it. Even where the scriptural world-view is concerned "neither by logical reasoning nor by intuition can man do more than take to himself the revelation of God on the authority of God."[7] Moreover, as Van Til never tires of reiterating, the facts of the world will not help to separate the true world-picture from the false, since they are not "brute" or "neutral": the non-Christian will invariably pervert them in his unbelieving direction.

The conclusion is inescapable: if everyone without exception has colored glasses cemented to his face, no one can criticize another person's spectacles, or indeed the "spectacle" of another world-view. Suddenly Tlön and the New Jerusalem become interchangeable, along with an infinite number of other resting places (e.g., "dialectical materialism, anti-Semitism, Nazism").

"Ah, but sovereign grace, the revelation of God in Holy Scripture, and the work of the Holy Spirit preserve us from these horrifying options, as well as from Tlön itself," comes the reply. Which brings us to our next parable.

---

[7]Van Til, *A Christian Theory of Knowledge,* p. 37

Worlds in Collision

If at this point our opponents smile and intimate that Christianity is, therefore, according to our own notion of it, simply a matter of irrational choice, we need not worry too greatly. For . . . it follows that our opponents as well as ourselves have chosen a position. We have chosen to follow full-fledged Christianity at all costs, while they have chosen to follow the "scientific method" at all costs.

Yet there is even so a difference between the two choices that are made. The choice we have made, we claim, is based upon the fact that we have first been chosen of God, while the choice our opponents have made, they claim, is made entirely by themselves.

Still further we have become aware of the fact that we are chosen of God only after accepting the truth of Christianity from the Bible. Thus the Bible appears at the outset to us as the absolute authority by which we seek to interpret life.[8]

The first point about a truly Protestant or Reformed doctrine of Scripture is that it must be taken exclusively from Scripture. It is, says Bavinck, exclusively from the Scriptures that we learn about Christ and his work of redemption for man. From the Scriptures alone do we learn about God's work of redemption for man. On its authority as the Word of God do we know the whole "system" of Christian truth. Therefore, also, on its authority alone do we believe what the Scripture says about itself.[9]

Van Til's conception of the noetic effects of sin has just been viewed in the light (or better, darkness) of Tlön; now we shall see how his effort through sovereign election, bibliology, and pneumatology to preserve his Reformed position from solipsistic collapse fares in contact with the Shadoks and the Gibis.

We refer to two engaging peoples conceived by Jacques

---

[8]Van Til, *Christian Theistic Evidences* (class syllabus, Westminster Theological Seminary, Philadelphia, Pa., 1961), p. 53

[9]Van Til, *A Christian Theory of Knowledge*, pp. 25–26.

Rouxel and drawn in the form of animated cartoons by J. F. Borredon for French national television (the ORTF).[10] The essence of the story is as follows: Once a very long time ago, the expanse of the heavens exhibited the earth in the center, and two worlds on either side of it. To the left was the planet Shadok, inhabited by Shadoks, and to the right, the planet Gibi, populated by Gibis. The planet Shadok had the unpleasant habit of changing its form without warning, which caused Shadoks to fall off; and the planet Gibi was long, thin, and virtually two-dimensional—much like a knife blade—and by pivoting as a teeter-totter does, it dumped many of its inhabitants whenever they collected at either end of it. Because of the undesirable condition of their home planets, both Shadoks and Gibis conceived the plan of moving to the earth. However, being totally opposed in appearance, temperament, and goals, they constituted an irrevocable threat to each other. The story of their humorous efforts to beat each other in the conquest and colonization of earth serves as the theme of this delightful television serial.

Like *Alice in Wonderland,* the story of the Shadoks and the Gibis operates on two levels: a simple child's plane of external action, and a more profound, philosophically relevant, adult level. Suppose that, consistent with their total mutual opposition of life-styles, the Shadoks and the Gibis enter into apologetic argument (we could hardly call it dialogue!) in an effort to convince each other of the truth of their respective views. The two positions are logically incompatible, and so both of them cannot be true (though they can both be false—a possibility not seriously entertained by either protagonist, however). Each position is formally similar to the other and thoroughly presupposi-

---

[10]The early portions of the Shadok-Gibi saga have been made available in book form: J. Rouxel & J.F. Borredon, *Les Shadoks et les Gibis* (Paris: Julliard, 1968).

tionalist (since a Shadok always starts from his world-perspective and a Gibi from his). Shadoks have their doctrine of election (Election-Sh), their inerrant Scripture (Bible-Sh), and their self-attesting inward experience of salvation produced by the immanent work of their God (Holy Spirit-Sh); Gibis affirm their opposing religious tenets on the basis of similar claims (Election-G, Bible-G, and Holy Spirit-G).

Both Shadoks and Gibis appeal, when pressed, to the facts of their world as supporting their religious claims in general and their revelation claims in particular; but neither is willing to make such facts a final test of truth. "For," they are frequently heard to say in religious discussions, "a fact cannot be brute or neutral; my evidence—or anyone else's, for that matter—cannot attain the status of 'fact' at all until one commits himself unreservedly to the true God." The "true God" refers, of course to God-Sh or God-G, depending on who is stating his case at the moment.

Sometimes the arguments reach a very high level of apologetic sophistication, as in the following instance:

Shadok: You will never discover the truth, for instead of subordinating yourself to revelational truth (Bible-Sh), you sinfully insist on maintaining the autonomy of your fallen intellect.

Gibi: Quite the contrary! [He repeats exactly the same assertion, substituting (Bible-G) for (Bible-Sh).] And I say what I have just said *not* on the basis of my sinful ego, but because I have been elected by God (Election-G).

Shadok: Wrong again! [He repeats precisely the same claim, with the simple substitution of (Election-Sh) for (Election-G).] Moreover, the sovereign election of which I am the unworthy recipient has been sealed by the very work of God the Holy Spirit (Holy Spirit-Sh). And all of this is clearly taught in the self-validating Scripture of our people (Bible-Sh), which, I should not have to reiterate, derives from the true God (God-Sh), not from sinful, allegedly autonomous man.

Gibi: How you invert everything. [He laboriously repeats the preceding argument, carefully employing (Holy Spirit-G), (Bible-G), and (God-G).]

Shadok: Absurd! The inevitable result of your colored glasses!

*Gibi:*It is *you* who have the glasses cemented to your face. Mine have been made transparent though sovereign grace (Election-G), as proclaimed by God's Word (Bible-G).

Shadok: Your religion is but the inevitable by-product of sin—a tragic effort at self-justification through idolatry. Let us see what God (God-Sh) *really* says in his Word (Bible-Sh).

Gibi: I will not listen to your alleged "facts." Unless you start with the truth, you have no business interpreting facts at all. Let me help you by interpreting the facts *revelationally* (Bible-G).

Shadok: Of course you will not listen to the proper interpretation of facts. Blinded by your sin, you catch each fact as you would a ball—and then you throw it into a bottomless pit!.[11]

Gibi: That's what *you* do with what *I* say—a clear proof of your hopeless, pseudo-autonomous condition. May the sovereign God (God-G) help you!

Shadok: May the true God (God-Sh) help *you!!*

The hopelessness of this encounter should be painfully evident. Neither viewpoint can prevail, since *by definition* all appeal to neutral evidence is eliminated. Even if it is admitted that facts can be known by the opposition, this admission is rendered totally valueless because correct *interpretation* of facts, as bearing on the ultimate truth of

---

[11]An analogy frequently appealed to by Van Til. Cf. *A Christian Theory of Knowledge*, p. 297.

the religious claims in question, rests only with the one who has seen the total picture by revelation (Bible-Sh? Bible-G?).

That this impasse is not simply a humorous *affaire Shadok-Gibi* stands forth in all its stark horror whenever a Christian presuppositionalism confronts a non-Christian presuppositionalism. Such was the case at the 1969 Wheaton College Philosophy Conference, where the final session was devoted to a paper on "Hegel, Marcuse, and the New Left."[12] The essayist, Bernard Zylstra of the Institute for Christian Studies in Toronto, had obtained his doctorate at the Free University of Amsterdam and represented the Dooyeweerdian variety of presuppositional Calvinism. Like Van Til's apologetic, this view rejects all "pretended autonomy of philosophical thought"—including the neutral investigation of factual evidence for religious truth-claims—and maintains that the "biblical basic motive is the only possible starting-point" of right thinking.[13]

Now it just so happens that Marcuse, in dependence on Hegel, is equally opposed to factual "neutralism"—but on the ground that all right thinking must begin from dialectic presuppositions ("philosophy originates in dialectic; its universe of discourse responds to the facts of an antagonistic reality"[14]) and must involve passionately subjective commitment to the radical and revolutionary alteration of a non-ideal, repressive status quo ("inasmuch as the struggle for truth 'saves' reality from destruc-

---

[12]November 7, 1969.

[13]Herman Dooyeweerd, *In the Twilight of Western Thought: Studies in the Pretended Autonomy of Philosophical Thought* (Philadelphia: Presbyterian and Reformed Publishing Co., 1960), p. 43

[14]Herbert Marcuse, *One-Dimensional Man: Studies in the Ideology of Advanced Industrial Society* (Boston: Beacon Press, 1964), p. 125.

tion, truth commits and engages human existence"[15]). To allow objective, factual verification to serve as a court of appeal is "to be satisfied with the facts, to renounce any transgression beyond them, and to bow to the given state of affairs"; it is thus to abrogate the revolutionary frame of reference essential to all genuine truth-seeking.[16]

How does our Dooyeweerdian critic handle such a viewpoint? By showing (1) that factual evidence is necessarily employed by everyone, Hegelian, Christian, or what have you, to evaluate alternative reality-claims in all areas of life? (2) that the facts do *not* support a dialectic-revolutionary *Weltanschauung?* and (3) that there *is* compelling factual support for the Christian affirmation that "God was in Christ, reconciling the world unto himself" (2 Cor. 5:19)? Not at all. Listen to what Zylstra does say:

> The scientist and the philosopher—Marcuse asserts—cannot deal with any supposedly neutral fact "outside" of the human "mind" unless he views it in its meaningful context. I agree with Marcuse up to this point, though the ultimate context from which "facts" derive their meaning-coherence will be radically different for him than it is for me. Marcuse is a Marxian humanist; I am a Christian.[17]

Thus the irresistible force meets the immovable object; the Shadok confronts the Gibi. Without prior commitment to the *truly* "meaningful context" of fact, facts are not compelling. But which "context"—the Christian or the Marcusean?

---

[15]*Ibid.*

[16]Herbert Marcuse, *Reason and Revolution: Hegel and the Rise of Social Theory,* 3rd ed. (Boston: Beacon Press, 1960), p. 27

[17]Bernard Zylstra, "Hegel, Marcuse, and the New Left" (mimeographed lecture, Wheaton College Philosophy Conference, Wheaton, Ill., November 7, 1969), p. 6.

By definition, this fundamental question can hardly be answered by an appeal to factual evidence, or the argument comes full circle! Claims by one side or the other to the possession of a higher level of internal consistency (with accompanying efforts to demonstrate inconsistency in the opponent's views) will hardly fill the bill either, for neither side allows a "neutral" standard of consistency to be imposed on his position from without. Even if he did, he would be faced with the disquieting existence of numerous fully consistent, but wholly psychopathic world-pictures (as created, for example, by paranoids and others who suffer from autistic derangements and build comprehensive world-views without reference to the facts of the world). And should Christian or Marcusean appeal in the most general sense (as is often done in tight argumentative situations) to his particular "context of interpretation" as "offering the fullest and best picture of universal reality" (the phraseology of course varies stylistically from apologist to apologist), circularity is by no means transcended, for if one does not mean by this that one's view can be judged by the (neutral) facts of "universal reality" in the public marketplace of ideas, one is simply reaffirming the way the universe looks *after* faith commitment to the metaphysic in question.

Van Til rejects the fact-oriented alternative, thereby eliminating in principle the possibility of his opponents' marshaling evidence against Christian claims. But the victory is entirely pyrrhic, for by accepting aprioristic circularity, he at the same time eliminates all possibility of offering a positive demonstration of the truth of the Christian view. Even Van Til's trenchant decimations of non-Christian positions are rendered ineffective by his ultimate presuppositionalism, since, like Marcuse, all the non-Christians whom Van Til chooses to criticize could employ his own two-edged sword against him, crying (in good Shadok-Gibi fashion): "Such criticisms are irrelevant, for right reason—true interpretation of fact and genuine application of the standards of consistency—begins with commitment to *my* presuppositional starting point!" And even if it were possible in some fashion to destroy all existent alternative world-views but that of orthodox Christianity, the end result would still not be the necessary truth of Christianity; for in a contingent universe, there are an *infinite* number of possible philosophical positions, and even the fallaciousness of infinity-minus-one positions would not establish the validity of the one that remained (unless we were to introduce the gratuitous assumption that at least one *had* to be right!).

When world-views collide, an appeal to common facts is the only preservative against philosophical solipsism and religious anarchy. Perhaps such results would be tolerable if the conflicts were restricted to Shadoks and Gibis, but when the issue concerns the truth of God in Christ versus soul-destroying options such as Hegelianism, Marxism, and Marcuse's philosophy of total societal upheaval, the stakes are simply too high to operate presuppositionally. Non-Christian positions must be destroyed factually and the Christian religion established factually. Any lesser procedure is the abrogation of apologetic responsibility to a fallen world.

AN ANCIENT APOLOGETIC PARABLE

Whence arise the presuppositional difficulties underscored by the fable of Tlön and the story of the Shadoks and the Gibis? Still another parabolic narrative offers an answer, for it accurately describes the character of the apologetic situation—a situation which is fundamentally misconceived by the aprioristic apologist. Early in the ninth century, a Syrian theologian and bishop of Harran in

Mesopotamia, Theodore Abu Qurra, wrote a treatise on God and the true religion.[18] In it is contained a parabolic treatment of the situation faced by the Christian apologist, and the parable warrants the closest attention.

A great king (God) had a son (mankind) who had grown up out of contact with his father. While journeying in a distant province the son fell seriously ill. The doctor accompanying him (reason) was incapable of treating the disease, but the king, learning of his son's plight, sent instructions (the gospel) for the healing of the boy. However, the king's numerous enemies also discovered what had happened, and they likewise sent remedies—purporting to come from the king—which were actually poisonous (non-Christian religious and philosophical options). The son's solution to this dilemma was to evaluate the remedies by three tests: first, what each remedy revealed about his father (comparison being made with the likeness to the father possessed by the son himself); second, how accurately each remedy pictured the nature of the disease; and thirdly, how sound the various curative methods appeared to be. With the help of the doctor, the son finally made his decision in terms of the remedy that best satisfied all three tests.

Now one may smile at the naivete of a test such as the first (sad to say, the son might easily evaluate the competing pictures of his father on the basis of his own sinful condition, rather than on the basis of the paternal imprint—the image of God—in his own person); but the general outlines of the parable are a most accurate representation of the character of the apologetic task. Abu

---

[18]This work is unfortunately not available in English, but appears in German. See Theodore Abu Qurra, *Traktat. Ueber d. Schöpfer und d. wahre Religion*, trans. and ed. George Graf von Hertling ("Beiträge zur Geschichte d. Philosophie d. Mittelalters," Vol. 14, No. 1; Münster i.W: Aschendorffsche Verlh., 1913).

Qurra, having had contact with Muslim proselytizing, saw clearly what the presuppositional apologist so often forgets: that the religious situation is *pluralistic*. Fallen man is not confronted with but one alleged message from the Father; he hears a cacophony of conflicting religious claims. What is he to do?

He cannot very well try all the various remedies in an arbitrary fashion, for all except the true remedy are poisonous in varying degrees, and his constitution could not possibly tolerate the infinite number of experiential trials necessary. But the apologetic presuppositionalist, as we have seen, cuts off all opportunity to determine the truth-value of competing religious remedies prior to the acceptance of one of them as a first principle of all meaningful thinking.

Thus the non-Christian is not left "without excuse" in the face of gospel proclamation. He can legitimately "excuse" himself from commitment to Christ on the ground—actually provided for him by the Christian apriorist!—that since no facts can be properly evaluated as evidence for a position without prior acceptance of that position, Christianity can have no more claim to his life than the infinite number of competing views that demand faith in *them* as the necessary condition for discovering "the truth." Theologically, one enters the cloud-cuckooland of fideism, which borders the philosophical realm of solipsism, where an infinite number of doors open to the gods of Tlön, Gibi, and Shadok.

But what apologetic alternative is available? That of the apostles and of the Lord Himself, who continually employ the de facto, *historisch* character of revelatory events (how attractively Van Til stresses such objectivity as opposed to Barthian dialectic evasions of it!) as offering "many infallible proofs" of the truth resident in the gospel. Our apologetic should be modeled on the Christ who

offered objective evidence of His power to forgive sins by
healing the paralytic and who convinced unbelieving
Thomas that He was God and Lord by the undeniable
presence of His resurrected body.[19]

With the apostle Paul, we must become all things to all
men. We must operate on the non-Christian's territory,
even as our Lord was willing to incarnate Himself in our
alien world. We must declare to the Agrippas of our day,
"The king knoweth these things, before whom also I
speak freely: for I am persuaded that none of these things
are hidden from him; for this thing was not done in a
corner" (Acts 26:26). The evidence of Christianity's truth
has never been closeted in a presuppositional corner; it
has always been in the public domain, capable of examination by all. As such, it must be brought to bear apologetically on the unbeliever, so that he will indeed stand naked,
without excuse, under the sheer pressure of incarnational
fact.

What does this kind of apologetic entail? First, a recognition that everyone—non-Christian as well as Christian—must employ inductive procedures to distinguish
fact from fiction.[20] Second, the realization that both those
out of relation with God and those in proper relation to
Him can compare alternative interpretations of fact and
determine on the basis of the facts themselves which
interpretation best fits reality.

It is noteworthy that when Adam heard the Lord's
voice calling to him after the Fall, he was still able to

---

[19]See Montgomery, *Where is History Going?* reprint ed. (Minneapolis:
Bethany, 1972), *passim;* "The Theologian's Craft: A Discussion of Theory
Formation and Theory Testing in Theology," in his *Christianity for the
Tough-Minded* (Minneapolis: Bethany, 1970), pp. 267–313; and "The Place of
Reason in Christian Witness" (ch. 1 of the present work).

[20]Cf. Georg Henrik Von Wright, *The Logical Problem of Induction,* 2nd ed.
(Oxford: Blackwell, 1957).

interpret properly both the origin of the voice and its meaning; the Fall did not render Adam incapable of comprehending a word from God. Had it done so, subsequent divine revelation would have been impossible in principle, and the heretical view of Matthew Flacius would have been vindicated: sin would actually have altered human nature and made man something other than man!

Third, one must see that acceptance of the heuristic assumptions of inductive method does not commit one to a scientistic metaphysic or denigrate God's revelation. What it does do is open up the possibility of distinguishing true revelation from false, the New Jerusalem from Tlön, and the king's remedy from the poisonous drugs of his adversaries.[21]

Fourth, when the non-Christian rejects the factual case for Christianity, he must not be allowed to justify himself by his alien starting point. Rather, he must be led to see that in all spheres other than that of Christian claims he regularly accedes to comparable evidence—and *has* to do so to retain meaningful knowledge of the past and operating existence in the present. Thus the non-Christian is driven to recognize the volitional nature of his rejection of Christ and his consequent moral responsibility for such unfaith. Apologetics fulfills its function only when it brings the unbeliever to the "offense of the cross," that is, to the cross as evidentially compelling and able to be resisted only by a deliberate act of egocentric will.

Finally, apologetics must never be confused with systematic theology. This is doubtless one of the chief roots of the misconception we have been discussing. Dogmatics is a field of endeavor directed to Christian believers and

---

[21]On the assumptions of scientific method versus the a prioris of the "Religion of Science," see Montgomery, *The Shape of the Past*, 2nd ed. (Minneapolis: Bethany, 1975), pp. 264ff.

thus properly begins with God's inerrant revelation of Himself in Holy Scripture. But apologetics is directed to *unbelievers*—to those who by definition do not accept God's Word as divine utterance. Here the focus must be on *their* needs, and the starting-point has to be the common rationality (the inductive and deductive procedures) that all men share. If we insist that non-Christians begin in our sphere of Christian commitment, we ask for the impossible and vitiate all opportunity of reaching them. Indeed, we devalue the very coinage of divine sovereignty that we are endeavoring to uphold, for we give the unbeliever the impression that our gospel is as aprioristically, fideistically irrational as the presuppositional claims of its competitors.

Could it ironically be that the wonderfully successful efforts of Calvin in the realm of dogmatics have sometimes led his followers to create the hydra of a "dogmatic" apologetic—an apologetic modeled on a deductive systematic theology? Whether this is an accurate judgment or not, there is no doubt that such apologetes as Van Til treat the non-Christian very much as if he were a Christian. Strange to say, this was also Karl Barth's method, though for very different reasons. In his treatment of Anselm, Barth describes his own approach when he says:

> Perhaps Anselm did not know any other way of speaking of the Christian *Credo* except by addressing the sinner as one who had not sinned, the non-Christian as a Christian, the unbeliever as believer, on the basis of the great "as if" which is really not an "as if" at all, but which at all times has been the final and decisive means whereby the believer could speak to the unbeliever.[22]

---

[22]Karl Barth, *Anselm: Fides Quaerens Intellectum*, trans. Ian W. Robertson (Richmond, Va.: John Knox Press, 1961), p. 71.

How very odd that Van Til, who, perhaps more than any other critic of Barth, has seen his universalistic tendency, was not thereby reminded that the apologetic approach to the unbeliever must be radically different from the systematic theologizing carried on by the believer. The non-Christian must not be presented with an a priori dogmatic; he must be offered the factually compelling evidence for the Christian truth-claim.

We call upon Van Til to carry further both his laudable stress on the objective character of divine revelation and his penetrating critique of Barthian dialectics. We call on him to see the genuine need of the non-Christian and declare to him concerning the incarnation of God in Christ, "This thing was not done in a corner"!

* * *

A new variant of reformed presuppositionalism has recently been put forth by Robert L. Reymond of the Covenant Theological Seminary, St. Louis, Missouri, in his monograph, *The Justification of Knowledge* (Nutley, N.J.: Presbyterian and Reformed Publishing Co., 1976). In an excellent review of this work, Dr. Robert H. Countess ventures the opinion that "if Reymond has done his work well, we may see a new era in apologetics—of a new void" (*Christianity Today*, November 18, 1977, pp. 34–35). Unfortunately, the book will not usher in a new apologetic era, for it holds to the basic philosophy of apriorism as developed by Van Til, Clark, and their followers.

However, Reymond *has* done his work well in recognizing a serious error in Van Til's approach which few presuppositionalists have admitted. He chides Van Til for not allowing adequate epistemological common ground between God and man: "The solution to all of Van Til's difficulties is to affirm, as Scripture teaches, that both

God and man share the same concept of truth and the same theory of language" (p. 105). Reymond properly sees that vertical communication between God and man and horizontal communication between believer and unbeliever depend upon the existence of such a common ground.

But once he admits that neither the sovereignty of God nor the fall of man militates against the use of human sensory and inferential functions to recognize factual reality—even when it is God who is speaking and acting—how can Reymond maintain a presuppositional stand? Does it not then become theoretically possible (as evidentialists hold) to insist that unbelievers face the de facto evidence in behalf of Christianity, and to argue that they are *irrational* (not just rationally consistent with their unprovable a prioris) if they do not?

Reymond's answer is that the non-Christian still need not shift his presuppositional stand, regardless of the evidence the Christian marshals, for the universe is so vast in extent that man can never know any given fact exhaustively. Thus the unbeliever can always come up with other possible explanations for any apologetic argument the believer presents to him.

Were this indeed a rationally sound course of action on the unbeliever's part, one wonders why the Lord bothered to offer miraculous evidence to the prophets of Baal, to those who questioned Jesus' ability to forgive the paralytic's sins, or to doubting Thomas—or why Paul bothered to catalog the witnesses to the resurrected Christ. The formal answer to Reymond's position is quite simple: though in a contingent universe anything is *possible,* neither Christian *nor* non-Christian can survive a single day of his life without acting on the basis of *plausibility,* not possibility. Even though the truck bearing down on you *could* be explained away in innumerable different fashions (e.g., it is a figment of your imagination), if you don't jump out of its path, you will be pronounced *irrational* (if not dead). Even though the evidence for Napoleon's existence *could* be discounted (as Bishop Whately did in his delightful *Historic Doubts*, showing that Hume's criticisms of the Gospel writers could reduce Napoleon to nonexistence), the student who depends upon such possibilities will certainly (not even possibly) fail his history course. And though the evidence for Jesus' life, death, and resurrection *could* be explained other than as Jesus Himself and the eye-witnesses to His career explained it, (e.g., Jesus could have been a Martian so cleverly disguised in a Jesus suit that no one could tell the difference), the man who tries to function in his ordinary life on the basis of comparable reasoning will soon be put away for his own protection. After all, the non-Christian himself might be a Martian cleverly dressed in a non-Christian suit; etc, etc.

In short, Reymond is right as to the common concept of truth and theory of language extending virtually from heaven to earth and horizontally across man's earthly experience; now he needs to take with more epistemological seriousness the historical revelation of God to man in this human sphere and the de facto incarnation of Christ which provides "many infallible proofs" in divine truth. The non-Christian can and must be led to see that the same inferential operations which he must use to survive in this world will, if applied to the evidence for divine revelation, lead to its acceptance as truth—and that any other conclusion is therefore irrational. Then if he still rejects the gospel, the real issue will be clear beyond all doubt: not consistently rational presuppositionalism, much less inadequate proof for Christianity, but willful refusal to bow to the God who factually has a claim on his life.

7

Lutheran Theology
and the Defense of
Biblical Faith

"Κριτήρια externa praemisimus ideo, quod animi hominum infidelium convertendorum iisdem praeparantur ad scripturam sacram, cum studio & desiderio discendi legendam atque meditandam. Cum enim universa gentilium, atheorum, & epicuraeorum gens non credat sacram scripturam a Deo esse profectam, eam legere vix dignatur. Quare necesse est, ut primo omnium per adducta externa κριτήρια, sive, ut alii vocant, signa & motiva credibilitatis, infideles moveantur, ut non improbabile esse censeant, sacram scripturam a Deo ducere originem, atque adeo eam aestimare, legere & meditari incipiant. Sic enim per κριτδ ήρια scripturae divinitus inspiratae interna ad fidem eidem adhibendam magis magisque permovebuntur, & per internum Spiritus sancti testimonium immota πληροφορία sive assensus fiducialis, quo scripturae adhaerescimus, accendetur, fovebitur, confirmabitur."

David Hollaz, *Examen theologicum acroamaticum* (Stockholm [Holmiae] & Leipzig, 1750), pp. 109–110.

STRANGE BEDFELLOWS

Can the truth of Christianity be "proven" to an unbeliever? Ought the Christian try to "demonstrate" the veracity of the gospel to the non-Christian? Should one attempt to "establish evidentially" the Bible's claim to be
the very Word of God? Here are two representative contemporary Lutheran judgments on these questions:

> The certainty of Christian faith is not dependent upon the
> demonstrable character of divine revelation. The idea that
> scientific studies and investigations should provide a solid
> foundation for faith and give it certainty is contrary to the
> nature of both science and faith. If this were indeed possi-
> ble, it would mean that science, within the empirical reality
> which is the object of its study, could discover something of
> that revelation of which faith speaks. The discoveries of
> science would in that case verify faith. But this would
> obviously be to ask something of science which it cannot
> give without ceasing to be scientific. Whether it be a ques-
> tion of a scientific investigation of nature or history, such a
> study cannot penetrate to that which is decisive for faith—
> the revelation of God.[1]

> Christian theology is the ability to exhibit, or preach, the
> Gospel, but not to prove it true by human arguments of
> reason or philosophy. As the Christian theologian pro-
> claims the truth, he wins souls for Christ, but not as he
> endeavors to prove true the mysteries of faith by principles
> of human reason. This also is the meaning of the axiom:
> "The best apology of the Christian religion is its proclama-
> tion." Let the Gospel be made known, and it will of itself
> prove its divine character. Christian apologetics has there-
> fore only one function: it is to show the unreasonableness
> of unbelief. Never can it demonstrate the truth with "entic-
> ing words of man's wisdom."[2]

[1]Gustav Aulén, *The Faith of the Christian Church,* trans. Wahlstrom and Arden
(Philadelphia: Fortress, 1948), p. 107; cf. pp. 95–96. (Rev. ed., Fortress, 1961.)

[2]J. Theodore Mueller, *Christian Dogmatics* (St. Louis: Concordia, 1934),
p. 71.

Only the presence of biblical citations in the second quotation and the absence of them in the first might suggest a difference in apologetic viewpoint on the part of these two theologians. The first statement derives from Gustav Aulén, the renowned spokesman for Lundensian theology, who categorically set himself against "biblicism" (the verbal inspiration and infallible authority of Holy Scripture)[3] and depreciated the substitutionary ("Latin," "Anselmian") doctrine of Christ's Atonement.[4] The second affirmation expresses the viewpoint of J. Theodore Mueller, the great Missouri Synod dogmatician, who throughout his long career stood fast for the inerrancy of Scripture and the Christology of the historic church, and vigorously opposed Lundensian theology as a Lutheran variant of reformed neoorthodoxy.

Yet the apologetic stance of these two Lutheran thinkers is virtually indistinguishable! Both claim that Christian revelation stands beyond proof and beyond demonstration—and that any attempt to offer an apologetic to establish its validity is to misunderstand the nature of the Christian gospel. As I have pointed out in chapter 1 and other writings, very much the same antipathy to positive apologetic argument is displayed throughout contemporary Protestantism: it has been equally characteristic of the old modernism, of the Barthian "crisis theology" that reacted against modernism, of Bultmannian existentialism, and of the orthodox Calvinism and pietistic fundamentalism which have fought the errors of liberalism, neoorthodoxy, and Bultmannianism.

The question we wish to pose in this essay is the difficult

---

[3] Aulén, *The Faith of the Christian Church,* pp. 81–85.

[4] Aulén, *Christus Victor* (New York: Macmillan, 1969), *passim.* For a critique see Montgomery, ed., *Chytraeus on Sacrifice* (St. Louis: Concordia, 1962), pp. 139ff.

but exceedingly important one concerning the proper relation between Lutheran faith and the apologetic task:
Ought the confessional Lutheran to feel the same antipathy toward the positive defense of the faith as is experienced by liberal Lutherans and non-Lutherans alike? Or
does Lutheran theology demand an apologetic for the
Word as aggressive as its proclamation of the Word?
Should orthodox Lutheranism share the antiapologetic
bed with contemporary theology, or have we inadver-
tently picked up the wrong room key altogether?

AN EXISTENTIAL LUTHER WITH
ARISTOTELIAN FOLLOWERS

We are told that, as those who go by Luther's name, we
should be the last to approach Christianity apologetically.
Jaroslav Pelikan, in his influential little monograph, *From
Luther to Kierkegaard,* maintains that the young Luther
had little interest in "natural theology"—in the knowledge of God or of divine truth which can be attained by the
sinner in his unregenerate state—and that even as an old
man when he did deal with the question, he orientated it
"around the concept of dread."[5] In other words, Luther's
fundamental approach was not objective, cognitive, factual, but rather existential: he approached truth questions, as Søren Kierkegaard would later, in terms of
dynamic, personal experience. We are told that Kierkegaard's aphorism that "truth is subjectivity" strikes
closer to Luther's world-view than any kind of objective
arguments for Christianity's validity. Was Kierkegaard
not expressing the spirit of Luther's position when he said
that to question or defend the truth of Christ is like a
husband seriously asking himself whether he could love

---

[5]Jaroslav Pelikan, *From Luther to Kierkegaard* (St. Louis: Concordia, 1950),
p. 23.

another woman—even to ask such a question labels his love as unreal?

Pelikan's sketch of the history of theological ideas between Luther and Kierkegaard presents essentially an arid territory of orthodox Lutheran dogmaticians who, while rejecting Aristotelian adulterations of the content of Christian theology, unwittingly incorporate Aristotelian philosophical methodology into their labors, thereby eventually corrupting Luther's existential insights and paving the way for the victory of rationalism. The stress on proofs for God's existence in such later orthodox dogmaticians as David Hollaz is clear evidence that Luther's disinterest in "natural theology" did not long remain among his followers.

One of the chief sources of Pelikan's interpretation, as evidenced by his own bibliographical notes, was the brief section on natural theology at the outset of Werner Elert's *Morphologie des Luthertums*. There Elert—who himself relies heavily on Ernst Troeltsch's *Vernunft und Offenbarung bei Joh. Gerhard und Melanchthon* (1891)—claims that Philipp Melanchthon inconsistently maintained in his *Apology to the Augsburg Confession* that "God can be known in no other way than through the Word," yet he "already accepted the essential elements of the later 'natural theology' " and "demonstrates the natural proofs of the existence of God."[6] From this point things went from bad to worse, both in Melanchthon himself and in the orthodox theologians of the next century and a half: Chemnitz, Gerhard, Calov, Hollaz, Baier. (Only Flacius deserves real praise, for he unqualifiedly condemned sinful man's *ratio*.) Tragically, dogmaticians

---

[6]Werner Elert, *The Structure of Lutheranism*, Vol. 1, trans. Walter A. Hansen (St. Louis: Concordia, 1962), p. 51. The English translation is preceded by revealing commendatory introductions by Pelikan and ALC theologian Robert C. Schultz.

such as these set forth positive apologetic arguments for
biblical truth, and the Lutheran astronomer-
mathematician Johann Kepler actually endeavored to
harmonize scientific discoveries with the Word of God!
"How far away from Luther we now are!" cries Elert, and
concludes:

> The development of "natural theology" is the march of
> history from Luther's primal experience *(Urerlebnis)* up to
> the Enlightenment. It ended with the ominous error that
> Christian faith in God and "natural knowledge of God" are
> essentially identical. For the naive apologists, for many a
> dogmatician, even for many a politician who wanted to
> "preserve religion for the people," this was a comfort and a
> satisfaction. For the church Philistine, as Tholuck ad-
> dressed him, it was reason for no longer knowing of an
> anguished conscience. But then came Ludwig Feuerbach.
> Then came Karl Marx and Nietzsche. They showed that
> the knowledge of "natural" man arrives at a totally differ-
> ent result. And when it came to the great test of the revela-
> tion of God's goodness, faithfulness, and mercy on land, at
> sea, and in the air—which Zöckler and many others
> taught—the result was decidedly negative. Was it surpris-
> ing that the generation of the war and the collapse declared
> the Christian belief in God to be a delusion because it had
> been refuted by the terrors and the fate that they had
> experienced?[7]

The Bultmannian and post-Bultmannian Lutherans of
our day carry this line of argument even farther. Does
Bultmann tear away all objective grounding for faith by
declaring that the ostensively historical descriptions of
our Lord's miraculous acts are really the mythological
garb in which the primitive church clothed its existential
experience of "authentic self-understanding"? Fine! In
this "one sees in unmistakable outlines the shadow of

---

[7]*Ibid.*, pp. 53, 57–58.

Luther,"[8] for Bultmann is removing the objective, intellectual props by which modern man may attempt to "justify himself," even as Luther removed the props of moral works-righteousness from sixteenth century man. Bultmann thus continues Luther's task of stripping away all the externals from faith—leaving it as it really is, a naked leap which can never be aided, much less established, by objective evidence or factual demonstration. This viewpoint has been expressed with particular forcefulness by such post-Bultmannian advocates of the new hermeneutic as Ernst Käsemann:

> Neither miracle nor the canon nor the Jesus of history is able to give security to our faith. For our faith there can be no objectivity in this sense. That is the finding which New Testament scholarship has made plain in its own fashion. But this finding is only the obverse of that acknowledgment which Luther's exposition of the third article of the Creed expresses.[9]

In sum, Luther's central conviction that a man is justified by grace through faith and his concomitant refusal to confuse law with gospel supposedly eliminated for him, if not objective grounds for faith, at least all uses of objective evidences in "defending" the faith. Luther's immediate followers, however, allegedly returned like the dog to its Aristotelian vomit in endeavoring to establish the truth of faith and to convince others of its veracity by objective argument. Such argumentation is foreign to true Lutheran belief, we are told, and must be excised as a cancer.

---

[8]Robert Scharlemann, "Shadow on the Tomb," *Dialog,* Vol. 1 (Spring, 1962), pp. 22–29.

[9]Ernst Käsemann, *Exegetisch Versuche und Besinnungen,* Vol. 1, 2nd ed. (Gottingen, 1960), p. 236.

LUTHER AND THE CLASSICAL
DOGMATICIANS REVISITED

Energy, existential or otherwise, need not be expended here in refuting the contention that Luther had no objective grounding for his faith. Merely his affirmation at Worms—"I am bound by the Scriptures that I have adduced, and my conscience has been taken captive by the Word of God"—should be enough to show that for Luther truth was hardly "subjectivity." For those interested in a detailed analysis of this issue, a previous essay of mine should prove useful.[10] Our task here is the more specialized one of determining to what extent Luther's theology allows for and encourages the *apologetic use* of Christianity's factual character in setting the faith before an unbelieving world. Granted that for Luther God's Word was objectively true; does it follow that its truth can be established and defended in the marketplace of ideas, or is the sinful character of the human situation an absolute barrier to such an operation? This is the question before us—and we shall now take it up (not forgetting, however, the sobering consideration that the strongest opponents of a Lutheran apologetic are those who base their antiapologetic stance on the conviction that Christianity is, after all, nonobjective!).

Even the reading of Pelikan leaves us a bit shaky as to the dichotomy between an allegedly existential Luther and his Aristotelian-apologetic followers. In Luther, admits Pelikan, "we do have at least one passage in which he expounds what virtually amounts to an argument [for God's existence] from the analogy of being. The detailed

---

[10]Montgomery, "Luther's Hermeneutic vs. the New Hermeneutic," *In Defense of Martin Luther* (Milwaukee: Northwest Publishing House, 1970), pp. 40–85. For other publications of this essay in English, and for published versions in German and French, see the "Acknowledgments" *ibid.*, p. 10.

commentary on Genesis, our chief source for the old Luther, deals with natural theology several times."[11] But this apologetic emphasis is attributed to "the old Luther"—not to the Reformer in his theological prime.

We could answer with E. M. Plass that Luther's Genesis commentary comprises the "longest and, in many respects, the maturest of his lectures."[12] However, this approach is unnecessary, for, as Luther scholars such as Philip S. Watson have shown, the Reformer's concern with natural theology was by no means limited to his later years. As early as 1525, Luther is expressly teaching in *The Bondage of the Will* that "the knowledge of predestination and of God's prescience has been left in the world [after the Fall] no less certainly than the notion of the Godhead itself."[13] In his Galatians commentary (1531)—considered by many to be the greatest of all Luther's writings—he condemns all attempts by the sinner to justify himself on the basis of the natural knowledge of God, while at the same time stoutly defending the existence of such natural knowledge and encouraging the Christian to dispute intelligently with unbelievers on the basis of it:

When you are to dispute with Jews, Turks, Papists, Heretics, etc., concerning the power, wisdom, and majesty of God, employ all your intelligence and industry to that end, and be as profound and as subtle a disputer as you can.[14]

Such arguments [arguments for divine truth based on human and earthly analogy] are good when they are

---

[11]Pelikan, *From Luther to Kierkegaard*, p. 22. The Genesis commentary references are to be found in *WA*, Vol. 42, pp. 291–92, 374.

[12]E.M. Plass, ed., *What Luther Says* (St. Louis: Concordia, 1959), Vol. 3, p. 1618.

[13]*WA*, Vol. 18, p. 618.

[14]Luther's comment on Galatians 1:3.

grounded upon the ordinance of God. But when they are taken from men's corrupt affections, they are naught.[15]

Though all efforts at self-salvation through natural theology must be unqualifiedly condemned, Luther sees the natural knowledge of God and of His law inscribed on every man's heart as the point of contact—the common ground—which makes the evangelistic task possible.

If the natural law were not written and given in the heart by God, one would have to preach long before the conscience were smitten. One would have to preach to an ass, horse, ox, or cow for a hundred thousand years before they accepted the law, although they have ears, eyes and heart as a man. They too can hear it, but it does not enter their heart. Why? What is wrong? Their soul is not so formed and fashioned that such a thing might enter it. But a man, when the law is set before him, soon says: Yes, it is so, he cannot deny it. He could not be so quickly convinced, were it not written in his heart before.[16]

P. S. Watson summarizes the case in the best traditions of dry Oxbridge humor:

He [Luther] had, after all, read his New Testament; and the first two chapters of the Epistle to the Romans, along with other passages dear to the natural theologians, could not escape his notice. He had, furthermore, too much reverence for the sacred text to ignore such passages, or to dismiss them as unimportant.[17]

---

[15]Comment on Galatians 3:15. Cf. Luther's *Tischreden* assertion that he found Cicero's teleological argument for God's existence very moving.

[16]*WA*, Vol. 16, p. 447.

[17]P.S. Watson, *Let God Be God!* (London: Epworth, 1947), p. 84. See also Paul Althaus, *Die Theologie Martin Luthers*, 2nd ed. (Gütersloh, 1963), ch. 3.

However, retorts the antiapologetic Lutheran, does this really penetrate to the heart of Luther's position? Granted that he held to natural knowledge of God; he nonetheless refuses to allow such knowledge a place in salvation. As specialists on Luther's view of "reason" have pointed out (one thinks especially of B. A. Gerrish[18] and Robert H. Fischer[19]), Luther indeed encourages rational operations in the secular realm (the earthly kingdom) but categorically rejects reason as a normative rule in the realm of salvation (the spiritual kingdom). Reason must never be allowed to govern or restrict God's Word; where this occurs, reason becomes Frau Hulda and Madam Jezebel—the Devil's whore.

> The Kingdom of Reason embraces such human activities as caring for a family, building a home, serving as a magistrate, and (as Rörer's MS. adds) looking after cows. All that can be demanded of me by God in such a sphere of activity is that I should 'do my best'. The important thing not to overlook is that this Kingdom has its boundaries; the error of the sophists is that they carry the saying 'to do one's best' *(facere quod in se est)* over into the *regnum spirituale,* in which a man is able to do nothing but sin. In outward affairs or in the affairs of the body man is master: 'He is hardly', as Luther drily remarks, 'the cow's servant.' But in spiritual affairs he *is* a servant or slave, 'sold under sin'. "For the Kingdom of Human Reason must be separated as far as possible from the Spiritual Kingdom."[20]

And what possible good can an apologetic do when, in Luther's thinking, natural knowledge of God offers no

---

[18]B.A. Gerrish, *Grace and Reason* (Oxford: Clarendon Press, 1962).

[19]R.H. Fischer, "A Reasonable Luther," *Reformation Studies: Essays in Honor of Roland H. Bainton,* ed. F.H. Littell (Richmond, Va.: John Knox, 1962), pp. 30–45.

[20]Gerrish, *Grace and Reason,* pp. 72–73.

substitute whatever for the Word of God in Jesus Christ?
Knowledge of the *Deus absconditus* can only impart terror; the *Deus revelatus*—God in Christ—offers the sole
avenue to peace and salvation, and He is accessible, not to
reason and demonstration, but to the eyes of faith. Thus
even Christ's miracles did not convince those who would
not accept His Word: "When miracles are performed,
they are appreciated only by the pious."[21] One must come
in faith to the lowly Christ of the manger and there,
paradoxically, one will meet the divine Savior. Luther's
theology calls for proclamation of this truth, not for an
impossible defense of it which invariably appeals to the
"natural man" desiring to justify himself.[22]

Here we arrive at the core of the matter. Luther very
definitely distinguished two kingdoms, the earthly and the
spiritual, and in fact considered this distinction to be one
of the most valuable aspects of his theology.[23] But does
this distinction dichotomize the world into a secular realm
where reason and proof operate, and a spiritual realm
where evidence has no place? This is precisely the impression given by virtually all modern interpreters of
Luther. Especially revealing is Robert Fischer's declaration that for Luther "such insights ["reason, experience,
common sense"] operate in what would later be called the
phenomenal realm; they do not penetrate the
noumenal."[24] The use of the terms "noumenal" and

---

[21]*WA*, Vol. 25, p. 240 (a comment on Isa. 37:30).

[22]So Regin Prenter interprets Luther in *Spiritus Creator*, 2nd ed. (Copenhagen,
1946), especially chaps. 2 and 3. *Ratio* and *lex* are presented as "belonging
together"; faith is "in contrast to all *sensus*" (ie., to all "experience which relies
on that which can be observed in the visible world"); God's revelation in flesh as
the Christ "is placed in absolute opposition to our human *sensus* and *ratio*";
"theological epistemology" consists of the *transformation sensus* by the
Creator Spirit.

[23]*WA*, Vol. 38, p. 102 ("Defense against Duke George," 1533).

[24]Fischer, "A Reasonable Luther," p. 39.

"phenomenal" (borrowed from the Kantian critical philosophy, which is itself dependent upon a Platonic separation of the realm of "ideas" or "ideals" from the phenomenal world of sense experience) is most significant. Luther is painlessly being absorbed into the idealistic-dualistic frame of reference characteristic of virtually all contemporary Protestant thought. Why can neoorthodox and other varieties of current theology confidently hold to their "theological insights" while simultaneously accepting the most destructive judgments of biblical critics regarding alleged factual errors in the biblical material and the supposed historical unreliability of the scriptural accounts of our Lord's life? Simply because the (noumenal) truth of theological statements, we are told, is in no way dependent on the phenomenal, secular issues connected with biblical history. After all, the Bible conveys *religious*, not scientific or historical truth! "The Bible is not a textbook of science"; etc.

Is Luther to be assimilated to the Platonic-Kantian perspective? The answer will depend squarely on what kind of *connection* Luther saw between the two kingdoms. If he in fact kept them in water-tight compartments, then a positive apologetic originating in the secular realm could not in principle justify truths lying in the spiritual sphere. The mere fact of Luther's belief in a natural theology, in the sense previously shown, strongly suggests some kind of connecting link between the kingdoms in his thinking; but what precisely is the nature of the link?

Troeltsch (whom we have already met in passing as one of the sources of Elert and Pelikan's antiapologetic view of Luther) is best known in Reformation studies for his negative views of Luther's social ethic.[25] He claims that

---

[25]Expressed in his *Social Teaching of the Christian Churches* (the section dealing with "Protestantism"). Cf. K. Penzel, "Ernst Troeltsch on Luther," in *Interpreters of Luther: Essays in Honor of Wilhelm Pauck*, ed. Jaroslav Pelikan (Philadelphia: Fortress, 1968), pp. 275–303.

Luther's theology produced social quietism because Luther never connected the theological insights operative in his spiritual kingdom with the activities of the earthly kingdom. This allegation has been decisively refuted by George Forell, who shows that, in the first place, Luther's two kingdoms are connected as to origin, for "these two separate realms are ultimately both God's realms"; and, even more important, they are linked in practice by the individual Christian believer, who is a citizen of both simultaneously ("Luther explains that a point of contact between the secular realm and the spiritual realm exists in the person of the individual Christian").[26] A parallel vindication of Luther is needed epistemologically.

As the individual Christian unites the two kingdoms in his person, thereby bridging the sociological gap between them, so *the Incarnate Christ Himself* links the two realms epistemologically. The incarnational center of Luther's theology eliminates entirely the possibility of making him an advocate of "two-fold truth"—a kind of sixteenth-century Averroës. In the sharpest possible opposition to Platonic dualism—and to the related modern dichotomies of Kantianism and of Lessing's ditch between historical fact and absolute truth—Luther declares that Jesus Christ, in His own person, offers immediate access to God. One begins with the earthly and finds the heavenly. Luther's words should be carefully pondered in the final version of his Galatians commentary:

> Paul is in the habit of linking together Jesus Christ and God the Father so frequently: he wants to teach us the Christian religion, which does not begin at the very top, as all other religions do, but at the very bottom. Paul commands us to ascend on the ladder of Jacob, at the top of which God

---

[26]G.W. Forell, *Faith Active In Love* (Minneapolis: Augsburg, 1959). pp. 121, 149.

Himself is resting, and the feet of which touch the earth next to the head of Jacob (Gen. 28:12f.). Therefore if you would think or treat of your salvation, you must stop speculating about the majesty of God; you must forget all thoughts of good works, tradition, philosophy, and even the divine Law. Hasten to the stable and the lap of the mother and apprehend this infant Son of the Virgin. Look at Him being born, nursed, and growing up, walking among men, teaching, dying, returning from the dead, and being exalted above all the heavens, in possession of power over all. In this way you can cause the sun to dispel the clouds and can avoid all fear and all errors too. And this view of God will keep you on the right path.[27]

Luther insists that the search for God begin at the connecting link between earth and heaven which exists at the point of the Incarnation. There we find a genuine human being ("nursed and growing up," "dying") but also very God of very God ("returning from the dead and being exalted above all the heavens"). "Philosophy," which starts elsewhere, must be forgotten; absolute truth is available only here. Why does Luther concentrate relatively little on traditional proofs for God's existence (even though he considered such argumentation valid)? Because for him it did not constitute the proper point of departure:

If you begin your study of God by trying to determine how He rules the world, how He burned Sodom and Gomorrah with infernal fire, whether He has elected this person or that, and thus begin with the works of the High Majesty, then you will presently break your neck and be hurled from heaven, suffering a fall like Lucifer's. For such procedure amounts to beginning on top and building the roof before you have laid the foundation. Therefore, letting God do whatever He is doing, you must begin at the bottom and

[27]WA, Vol. 40, pt. 1, pp. 79ff. (published 1535 and 1538).

say: I do not want to know God until I have first known this
Man; for so read the passages of Scripture: "I am the Way,
the Truth, and the Life"; again: "No man cometh unto the
Father but by Me" (John 14:6). And there are more passages to the same effect.[28]

Luther is not antiapologetic; he is, rather, exceedingly
careful in his starting-point. The *point de départ* must be
Christ; in methodology one must "begin at the bottom"
with the Incarnation; and no reasoning (or anything else,
for that matter!) can be legitimately regarded as ground for
works-righteousness or self-justification.

Admittedly, Luther did not build a formal apologetic
from this incarnational starting-point. His task was not to
defend the soundness of the biblical history or of its picture of Christ. In the sixteenth century, no reputable
theologians of any school of thought questioned the veracity of the scriptural text. The cold winds of rationalistic
biblical criticism had not yet begun to blow. (To be sure,
Renaissance humanists such as Lorenzo Valla would later
be regarded as precursors of such criticism, but they
constituted no negative apologetic threat to biblical authority in Luther's time.) Luther often said that he did his
best work when angry; that is, he recognized that his
theological activities were determined in large part by the
contemporary pressures upon him. These pressures came
not from unbelievers doubting the authority of the Word
but from churchmen who misinterpreted it. Thus Luther's
battles were necessarily hermeneutic rather than apologetic in character.

Moreover, since he was especially confronted by the
traditional Romanist on the right and the fanatic
Schwärmer on the left, both of whom appealed to extra-

---

[28]*WA*, Vol. 36, pp. 61ff. (sermon of 6 Jan. 1532, on Micah 5:1).

biblical miracles in their midst, Luther preferred to fight on the common ground of the Word, emphasizing the truth—which must never be forgotten apologetically in our contingent world!—that those who *want* to discount the clear evidence of God's miraculous dealings can always find *some* way (improbable though it may be) of doing so.

But the fundamental themes of Luther's theology were most definitely hospitable to a positive apologetic and bore fruit apologetically when, not so many years later, the very authority of the Word came under fire. We have already stressed the central role the Incarnation played in Luther's thought—eliminating theological schizophrenia and offering a bridge from ordinary human experience to the divine truth of God's revelation. Related themes of great apologetic consequence in his theology include (1) his psychosomatic *holism* (Luther's refusal, in debate with Zwingli and others, to separate Christ's spirit from His body; he thereby avoided the trap of "spiritualist" theology which is in the last analysis unverifiable and indefensible—as was the claim of reformed modernists of our century that Christ rose from the dead "spiritually" but not necessarily in body)[29]; (2) Luther's constant epistemological insistence on the *objectivity* of Christian truth (his repeated assertions that to find the true meaning of the gospel one must always go from "the outward to the inward" and that the gospel lies entirely *extra nos* not only precluded subjectivism and auto-salvation, but also provided the foundation for the teaching of the orthodox Lutheran dogmaticians that *notitia*—objective fact—must always ground *fiducia*—personal, subjective commitment—and that Christian heart conviction can be

---

[29]See Montgomery, "Inspiration and Inerrancy: A New Departure," *Crisis in Lutheran Theology*, vol. 1, 2nd ed. (Minneapolis: Bethany, 1973), pp. 15–44.

justified by external evidence)[30]; (3) Luther's *sacramental teaching* (his firm maintenance of the *finitum est capax infiniti* principle places him most definitely outside the Platonist camp and opens the way to the widest variety of apologetic operations, since every fact in the world—"even the most insignificant leaf of a tree," to use Luther's own expression—becomes a potential avenue to Christ)[31]; and, (4) finally, his *inductive methodology* (Luther's requirement that one discover what Scripture is actually saying and not force it into alien categories—such as Zwingli's metaphysical speculations about the nature of "bodies"—made possible the defense of the faith in a world about to recognize the necessity of open, inductive, scientific procedure in the discovery of truth. Those who followed Luther's hermeneutic, as opposed to the deductive model of Ramist Calvinism, were thus—as in the case of Tycho Brahe and Kepler—at the forefront of both scientific advance and the apologetic reconciliation of Scripture and scientific discovery).[32]

Though not himself an apologist in the strict sense, Luther provided, through such theological insights, the basic orientation necessary for the apologetic emphases of the classical Lutheran dogmaticians. Elert finds it especially galling to admit that in regard to the efforts of the dogmaticians and Lutheran scientists such as Kepler to harmonize science and Scripture, "Luther had led the way with related interpretations of Genesis."[33] But is it not far more reasonable to see a positive relationship

[30]See Montgomery, "The Theologian's Craft," *Suicide of Christian Theology,* (Minneapolis: Bethany, 1970), pp. 267–313.

[31]See Montgomery, "Cross, Constellation, and Crucible," *In Defense of Martin Luther,* pp. 87–94.

[32]*Ibid,* pp. 94–113.

[33]Elert, *The Structure of Lutheranism,* p. 57.

between the apologetic activity of the great Lutheran theologians following Luther and the work of Luther himself, rather than to claim that somehow all of these theologians—who were evidently trying to be faithful to the great Reformer—somehow managed to pervert his theology by latching on to peripheral aberrations in his thought?

Even Elert and Pelikan have to admit that hardly a great name in Lutheran dogmatics from Luther's time to the eighteenth century disregarded "natural theology" and the objective defense of Christian truth. The following concise apologetic bio-bibliography should offer sufficiently intimidating evidence in this regard; the citations, taken together, constitute a veritable catalog of apologetic argumentation by the sixteenth- and seventeenth-century Lutheran fathers:

Chemnitz (1522–1586); *Loci theologici* (Frankfurt & Wittenberg, 1653), Pt. 1, pp. 19ff. ("De notitia Dei"); *Examen Concilii Tridentini,* ed. Preuss (Leipzig, 1915), pp. 6ff. ("De Sacra Scriptura").

Heerbrand (1521–1600): *Compendium theologiae* (Leipzig, 1585), pp. 33ff.

A. Hunnius (1550–1603): *Tractatus de sacrosancta maiestate, autoritate, fide ac certitudine Sacrae Scripturae* (Frankfurt, 1591), *passim.*

Hafenreffer (1561–1619): *Loci theological,* 3rd ed., (Tübingen, 1603), pp. 30ff.

Gerhard (1582–1637): *Loci theologici,* Vol. 1, ed. Frank (Leipzig, 1885), pp. 266ff. (on the question of God's existence), pp. 25ff. (on the authority, canonicity, and reliability of the biblical books).[34]

J. V. Andreae (1586–1654): *Sol veritatis sive religionis christianae certitudo*, in his *Rei christianae & literariae subsidia* (Tübingen, 1642), pp. 1–120. (The *Sol veritatis* is an abridgement of Hugo Grotius' *De veritate religionis christianae:* "commonly held to be the pioneer work in modern apologetics."[35])

Calov (1612–1686): *Systema locorum theologicorum* (Wittenberg, 1655–1677), loci on God (e.g., II, pp. 61–86) and Holy Scripture.

Quenstedt (1617–1688): *Theologia didactico-polemica*, I (Wittenberg, 1685), pp. 97–102 ("An per alia κριτήρια persuaderi possit Sac. Scripturae autoritas?"), 250ff. ("De Deo, ejusque naturali notitia").

Baier (1647–1695): *Compendium theologiae positivae*, ed. Walther, I (St. Louis, Mo., 1879), pp. 121–31 (catalog of arguments leading to *fides humana*, with references to apologetic arguments in still other dogmaticians of classical Lutheran orthodoxy—not included here for want of space—e.g., Huelsemann and Dannhauer).

Hollaz (1648–1713): *Examen theologicum acroamaticum* (Stockholm [Holmiae] ? Leipzig, 1750), pp. 106ff. (the

---

[34]An examination of these sections of Gerhard's *Loci* will reveal how wide of the mark is Robert Scharlemann's attempt, in his book, *Thomas Aquinas and John Gerhard* (New Haven, Conn.: Yale University Press, 1964) to relate Gerhard to Kant's critical philosophy, modern German existentialism, and Bultmannian theology by finding in him a dualistic separation between an alleged finite realm of formal, conceptual, objective knowledge and the realm of faith where only the "dialectical word" and "acoustic knowledge" hold sway (see especially pp. 28-37).

[35]J.H. Crehan, "Apologetics," *A Catholic Dictionary of Theology*, Vol. 1 (London, 1962), p. 117. On Andreae and his interest in Grotius' apologetic, see Montgomery, *Cross and Crucible: Johann Valentin Andreae (1586-1654), Phoenix of the Theologians*, Vol. 1 (The Hague: Nijhoff, 1971), pp. 42, 90–91.

external evidences of the divine origin of Holy Writ), 188ff. (the natural knowledge of God).[36]

It will be noted that these citations range across the entire period of Lutheran orthodoxy, beginning with the generation of Luther's and Melanchthon's own students. Moreover, the list could be readily extended by the addition of the names of exegetes such as Chytraeus (of whom Elert says sarcastically that he finds "in every chapter of the First Book of Moses the proof for one or more *loci* of dogmatics"[37]) and authors of works defending the Bible against charges of contradiction and error (e.g., Andreas Althamer, whose *Conciliationes locorum Scripturae* of 1527 went through at least sixteen editions).

But did these Lutheran apologists not inevitably weaken the biblical picture of man's total depravity, de-emphasize the scriptural teaching concerning the Holy Spirit's work in salvation, and introduce a subtle synergism into the preaching of the gospel of divine grace? Not at all. They recognized (though Elert seemed to have difficulty in doing so) that the Flacian alternative to the view that man retained his thinking and reasoning process after the Fall is nothing less than heresy; for if original sin meant the loss of the very image of God in man (including the loss of his rational faculty), man would have ceased to be man, no subsequent revelation could even in principle have been communicated to man, and Christ could not even have become man without becoming an irrational sinner! In retaining Luther's view of the Incarnation as the center of theology, the orthodox dogmaticians rightly opposed any Flacian attempt to dehumanize man by a con-

---

[36]Cf. J. Pelikan, "Natural Theology in David Hollaz," *Concordia Theological Monthly*, Vol. 15 (1947), pp. 253–63.

[37]Elert, *The Structure of Lutheranism*, p. 57.

cept of the Fall that would lead to a loss of man's ability to distinguish truth from falsehood in secular matters or (which is the same thing) to distinguish true from false claims that God was in fact incarnate in the secular sphere.

Nor did this apologetic approach produce a "depneumatized" theology. The dogmaticians rightly maintained that the *fides humana* or "historical faith" could not in itself save. *Notitia* is possessed by the devils also, who tremble but are not saved because of it. There must be the personal commitment—the commitment of the whole person—to Christ for salvation, and that is brought about solely by the Spirit's work. At the same time, however, the orthodox theologians correctly refused to say (as the modern neoorthodox do) that this personal commitment through the work of the Holy Spirit somehow "produces" the *notitia* or offers the only evidence of its reality. Hardly! The facts of God's existence and of His incarnate revelation in Jesus Christ stand as objectively true and evidentially compelling wholly apart from belief in them; faith in no sense creates their facticity. They stand over against man, judging him by their sheer veracity and compelling force—and unless he volitionally refuses to believe, and goes against all sound reasoning in so doing, they will move him to a Spirit-produced conversion and living relationship with Jesus Christ.

"Synergism"? Hardly, for everything is done by God, not by man. The evidential facts are God's work, and the sinner's personal acceptance of them and of the Person on whom they center is entirely the product of the Holy Spirit. To argue that the Lutheran dogmaticians fell into synergism because they defended the faith and expected a rational response from the sinner would require our condemning their *preaching* as well (and, indeed, all Christian preaching), on the ground that it presupposes a responsible decision on the sinner's part. But the same Paul who asserted unqualifiedly that men are saved by grace alone (Eph. 2:8, 9) told the Philippian jailer to "believe on the Lord Jesus Christ" (Acts 16:37) and defended God's truth in philosophical terms on the Areopagus (Acts 17) and cited historical evidence for Christ's resurrection in conjunction with his very statement of the nature of the gospel (1 Cor. 15). All appeals to the sinner, whether in evangelistic preaching, or in evidential argument, must assume the existence of rational faculties to permit communication at all; synergism exists only when, following conversion, the justified man is led to believe that in any way *whatever* (rational, moral, volitional) he contributed to his own salvation. Lutheran theology particularly—in comparison with other theological traditions—keeps the knife-edge of this mystery sharp, thereby making possible a most aggressive apologetic combined with a most salutary theocentrism.

AGONY IN SEARCH OF THE ECSTASY: THE TWENTIETH-CENTURY MISSION FIELD

And yet, our antiapologetic Lutheran offers his final counter: Surely the "defense" of Christianity violates the most fundamental aspect of Lutheran theology, the law-gospel principle! When arguments are offered for the truth of the Word, sinners are led, even when the apologist does not intend it, to rely upon themselves (the misuse of the law) rather than, in realization that *lex semper accusat,* to come to God solely on the ground of His free grace (the gospel).

Let me suggest, however, that the situation is the *exact reverse* of this: the neglect of apologetics is the surest way to *confuse* law and gospel, particularly in our day.

If we go back to the beginning of this essay, we find a strange phenomenon: the orthodox Mueller and the Lun-

densian Aulén occupying the same antiapologetic bed.
Both argue that "proof" is incapable of being marshaled
to justify their positions. One bases his beliefs on an
inerrant Scripture, the other upon an erring Scripture and
undefined elements in the church's heritage of faith. Note
that, under these conditions, an individual standing outside these two commitments has no way of "testing the
spirits" to see which view, if either, is worthy of *his*
commitment. "Begin with inerrant Scripture!" cries
Mueller. "Begin with my understanding of 'the faith of
the Christian Church'!" cries Aulén. In the absence of an
apology that will make sense to the uncommitted, it is
impossible, *even in principle,* to decide between these
views. But if this is where the religious question is left,
then the non-Christian will make an *arbitrary* decision—
which will be dependent on *himself alone* (not on evidence outside himself)—and his commitment (even if to
the true position) will be man-centered and therefore
legalistic. The neglect of an apologetic for Christian truth
thus inevitably confuses law with gospel by turning gospel
into arbitrary, self-centered law. Only a genuine apologetic based on external, objective fact as presented in general and special revelation preserves religious decision
from arbitrariness, keeps the gospel truly *gospel,* and (to
use Watson's felicitous phrase) "lets God be God."

Moreover, let us note well that the options before the
unbeliever today are by no means limited to a Mueller and
to an Aulén. Ours is an age of religious cacaphony, as was
the Roman Empire of Christ's time. From agnosticism to
Hegelianism, from devil-worship to scientific rationalism,
from theosophical cults to philosophies of process: virtually any world-view conceivable is offered to modern man
in the pluralistic marketplace of ideas.[38] Our age is indeed
in ideological and societal agony, grasping at anything and
everything that can conceivably offer the ecstasy of a

cosmic relationship or of a comprehensive *Weltanschauung*. Will Lutherans, having perhaps the strongest theological and apologetic resources in Christendom, continue to hide behind our traditions and our ecclesiastical structures, fearing the world of intellectual unbelief, or will we yield to the Holy Spirit—the Spirit of truth—who can overcome our inertia and bring us into the agoras of our time, there to establish by "many infallible proofs" the true character and message of the Unknown God?

---

[38]I have developed this point, over against the Reformed presuppositionalists Gordon Clark and Cornelius Van Til, in my essay "Gordon Clark's Historical Philosophy," *Where Is History Going?* (Minneapolis: Bethany, 1972) and "Once Upon an A Priori" (ch. 6 of the present work).

8
The Current Scene

TECHNOLOGY AND ESCHATOLOGY

While the astronauts of Apollo 16 were successfully carrying out their incredibly complex technical mission in 1972, a colloquy relating theology and technology was in full swing in Strasbourg, France. Co-sponsored by the renowned Faculty of Protestant Theology of the university, whose history began with John Calvin and Martin Bucer, and by Syracuse University's Religion Department, where the death-of-God movement originated, this conference brought together such noted speakers as Jacques Ellul, death-of-God-er Gabriel Vahanian, and hermeneutic specialist Hans-Georg Gadamer.

Among invited observers were a number of prominent theologians from both sides of the Atlantic. The international gamut ran from Bultmann critic Fritz Büri to the University of Chicago's Langdon Gilkey. Though ironically hobbled by a severe technical difficulty—the lack of simultaneous translation of French lectures into English for the benefit of monoglot Americans—the colloquy raised some exceedingly vital questions on the place of theological thinking in the modern technical age.

Secular specialists threw down their gauntlets before the theologians. Physicist Astier of the Ecole Polytechnique, Paris, lucidly summarized the technological world-view: the universe evolves from an original ball of gas; the "higher" aspects of human life must be understood in naturalistic terms—philosophical or religious quests for meaning (the Logos) are ultimately derived from sexuality, which in turn relates to the development of human consciousness; genetic mechanisms are the key to solving the problems of man and society.

Desroches, a sociologist of religion who earlier that year had participated in a dialogue with theology-of-hope advocate Jürgen Moltmann, refused to recognize any single eschatology or religious hope, for "religious hopes are many and varied—indeed, innumerable." He illustrated his thesis by messianic phenomena among the Congolese, the "cargo cults," and his specialty, the Shakers. All these display the four characteristics of religious eschatology: hope as "the dream of one who is wide awake" (citing Bossuet who in turn cited Aristotle); hope as "collective ideation"; hope as an "exultant expectation"; and hope as "generalized utopia."

Theological responses fell into two nicely distinguishable categories. The Americans were invariably the radicals, ringing the changes on secular, post-death-of-God theology. The Europeans offered a blend of essentially Barthian and post-Bultmannian alternatives.

Representative of the Americans were Vahanian and Miller of Syracuse. Vahanian, whose radicalizing of Barth brought the death-of-God theology into existence (though not to wide public notice) in 1961, argued that the polarization of the *novum* (progress) and the *eschaton* (the theological hope) can be overcome by radical apprehension of the Resurrection in the present moment. "The Resurrection is the decisive faith-event," he declared. On being asked whether this christological terminology could be dropped in favor of "existential moment" or "moment of perception," he agreed that "one can use any language one wishes" as long as "technology is invested with all its possibilities."

Miller did the only exegesis at the colloquy, but it was of the Greek poets rather than of the Bible. In his view, evidently, the God of Christianity might be dead, but not the Great God Pan. In a study of "Olympian mythology," Miller distinguished the Greek concepts of *techne* and *mechane* (the latter has divine overtones: the *deus ex machina*). His conclusion was that Asclepius offered the insight that technology needs to be grounded in the therapeutic consciousness of man's suffering. Gadamer would ground technology in ontology; Miller, in "psychology." Queried biologist Canguilhem, "I don't quite see how you get from the Asclepian vision to psychology." Miller: "By psychology I really meant poetry. I neglected to mention that *techne* relates to prophecy." For Vahanian and Miller, the Scriptures of Christianity and of Greek religion were similarly useful; they both offered mythological insights symbolically pertinent to the technological age.

Gadamer, in line with his acceptance of the post-Bultmannian hermeneutical circle that makes objective reality always a function of the present observer, called for "self-understanding" in technology and offered his ontological and immanent Word as a focal point for healing. The task of the theology is to "reinterpret the ordinary experiences of man by way of self-understanding regarded as an act of grace." Thus technology and the city can offer a way to truly human existence.

Keynote speaker Jacques Ellul did not share this optimism. In an address that in quality and attractiveness of presentation vastly outshone all other contributions, the Bordeaux legal scholar and polymath argued that technology solves only the problems it poses for itself, and these problems are themselves the result of technological pre-conditioning. Therefore, a vicious circle is created in which man is in danger of losing his true humanity. Here two choices face him: the modern theology that baptizes technology, thereby betraying man, and the historic Christian theology of a "revealed Transcendent" that gives man the perspective to subdue the earth.

"But why the one alternative rather than the other?" asked Gilkey. "Why must we choose the 'Transcendent'?" In line with his Barthian presuppositionalism, Ellul could only reply, "No justification of this choice is possible. You can't find a point of reference which isn't already in one system of commitment or the other."

This refusal to face the epistemological question was equally characteristic of the other Barthian speakers. Faessler of Geneva simply declaimed his position; Ricoeur laminated onto Barth. Although this theology was in many respects incompatible with other presuppositional views offered, Faessler could blithely declare, "One must reject all apologetics. *Credo ut intellegam.*"

To which sociologist Desroches directed the biting comment: "Any religionist can say that—Buddhist, Christian; Catholic, Protestant." Even Ellul, whose thinking was rightly characterized by Mehl of Strasbourg as "lucidity without compromise," could not hold the field simply by proclaiming a viewpoint.

In a pluralistic age of science, the Colloquy on Technology and Eschatology made crystal clear that theologies without apologetic strength and epistemological sophistication are easily dismissed by secularists whose disciplines demand evidence, not simply claims. The colloquy sessions took place in the university's Pasteur lecture hall. Some wished for a pasteurization of theology that would deliver it from the dual infections of secularism and apriorism.

HOW SCIENTIFIC IS SCIENCE?

For more than a quarter of a century the American Scientific Affiliation (ASA) has been relating scientific data to Christian convictions. Its twenty-seventh annual meeting, held in the labyrinthine halls of York University in suburban Toronto, endeavored to find a way through one of the great mazes in contemporary philosophy of science. Under the general subject "Presuppositions of Science: A Christian Response," participants struggled with the question, Do scientific advances actually bring about greater objective knowledge of reality, or do they merely signify the substitution of one metaphysical paradigm for another without necessarily moving closer to the real nature of things?

Two major sessions were devoted to the metaphysical versus objectivist view of scientific progress, and the issue spilled over into many other discussions. What made this inevitable was the strong representation of Calvinist presuppositionalists (Stanford Reid, Robert Knudsen) and Dooyeweerdians (Bernard Zylstra) on the program.

As might be expected, those who hold to an ultimately untestable theological starting-point find comfort in the notion that science may, after all, be dealing not with brute facts at all but with data that become "facts" as they are incorporated into particular scientific constructs. Thomas S. Kuhn's *The Structure of Scientific Revolutions,* which persuasively sets forth the metaphysical interpretation of scientific activity, is already paralleled in Calvinist-presuppositionalist circles by Gordon H. Clark's *Philosophy of Science and Belief in God.*

Reid, in his characteristically aggressive opening address, chastened the eighteenth-century Anglican apologists Berkeley and Paley and their ilk for trying to "prove Christianity rationally," thereby "adopting the rationalist's view of an autonomous universe."

In opposition to such a "pretended autonomy," Zylstra, of the Calvinist-Dooyeweerdian Institute for Christian Studies in Toronto, chided evangelicals such as Carl F.H. Henry and asserted that the "biblically inspired view of created reality can be given theoretical formulation in terms of Herman Dooyeweerd's reformational philosophy." Zylstra's attempts to show the application of Dooyeweerd to such pressing contemporary issues as territorial waters and airspace bewildered many conferees.

The same reaction accompanied the efforts of Knudsen, Van Til's successor at Westminster Seminary, to show how Dooyeweerdian method assists concept-formation in the special sciences. When, for example, Knudsen argued that our presuppositions as to what life is must precede our distinctions between the organic and the inorganic, I asked myself if I must follow the Dooyeweerdian path to distinguish my barber from the barber pole in front of his shop.

In contrast to these emphases came presentations by pathologist James Kennedy of Queens University, Herman Eckelmann of the Cornell University Space Center, and T. Harry Leith, professor of natural science at York. For Kennedy, "the scientist can gain knowledge about God by applying the same principles he uses in doing his research." Eckelmann (toward whom I admit an especially powerful bias, since he was instrumental in my conversion to Christianity while an obstreperous philosophy major at Cornell) maintained that the Van Tilian refusal to allow arguments for an infinite God or divine truth from finite scientific evidence is as illogical as would be the refusal to accept the description of an infinitely extensible line by a noninfinite mathematical formula. In a striking lecture relating the Genesis cosmology to the latest scientific speculation as to the origins of the solar system—a lecture illustrated by slides prepared at the Space Center—Eckelmann showed by example how much more fruitful it is to correlate empirical scientific fact with revelational truth than to win a Pyrrhic theological victory by refusing to admit the sure reality of scientific discoveries.

My Cornell philosophy mentor E. A. Burtt had not been wrong in stressing the "metaphysical foundations of modern science," for today's science often palms off unrecognized and nonscientific value judgments as empirical fact (the phenomenon Anthony Standen well captured in his phrase "science as a sacred cow"). Eckelmann nicely demonstrated, however, that the answer to this is not to reduce all science to metaphysics but to identify genuine empirical work as such and see it as a pathway to the confirmation of scriptural revelation.

Leith closely analyzed the Kuhn thesis and offered trenchant criticisms of his metaphysical interpretation of scientific revolutions. Having written his doctoral dissertation on Karl Popper, Leith was in a particularly good position to explicate Popper's rejection of Kuhn's argument. Popper rightly notes that the truly great scientific advances have been made not by the presentation of untestable world-views such as those of Freud and Marx (anything on the couch fits Freud; anything in history is absorbed by Marx), but by such *testable* theories as Einstein's (supported by the crucial Michelson-Morley experiment). In his banquet address on "Galileo and the Church," Leith offered a concrete illustration of how Christian faith must come to terms with the realities presented by science—and how revelational religion has nothing to fear and everything to gain by doing so.

EPISCOPAL FUTURITY AND FUTILITY

Of Anglicans can be said what Longfellow wrote of a certain little girl: when they are good they are very, very good (the Book of Common Prayer, Bishop Butler, Charles Williams, C.S. Lewis, John Stott), and when they are bad they are horrid (the Cambridge radicals, Bishop Robinson, Bishop Pike, Joseph Fletcher, Thomas Altizer). It was therefore with ambivalent feelings that I attended the Inaugural Symposium at Seabury-Western Theological Seminary in 1973, honoring the seminary's new president and dean, Armen Jorjorian, known in Episcopal circles for a creative institutional-chaplaincy program in Texas. The Right Reverend John E. Hines was on hand to preach, while "futurologist" Robert Theobald served as main speaker.

To everyone's surprise, Theobald appeared not in person but on videotape from Arizona to deliver his keynote address (and the moderator brought the house down by noting that this was being done "the Anglican way—*via media*"). Following the taped address, discussion groups met to pose questions to Theobald, and he answered them over a conference telephone circuit.

Theobald set forth his own approach of the future against the background of three other current views with which he strongly disagrees. First, there is the "positive extrapolist," such as Daniel Bell (*Work and Its Discontents*) who sees the future as a linear, positive extension and expansion of the present. This approach naively accepts a pro-Western doctrine of the inevitable progress of present technological society. In reaction, one encounters the "negative extrapolists" (the SDS mentality) who agree with the positive extrapolists that the future will consist of a larger-than-life present, but believe this will be an inferno, not a paradiso. Face to face with this overwhelming technological cacatopia, some opt out: the third futurology, an "intra-wordly mysticism" classically expressed by Charles Reich in *The Greening of America,* proclaims the gospel of "do your own thing" and expects some extraordinary mechanism to set things right.

For Theobald, a socio-economist by training, these three models of the future are hopelessly simplistic and fatalistic. A strong fan of science fiction, he shares its perspective of an open future, capable of multifaceted development.

In his recent work *An Alternative Future for America II* and his anthology *Futures Conditional,* Theobald maintains that we are entering a world where the goal-oriented Protestant work ethic is being replaced by a "process-orientation." No absolute and inevitable goals force mankind into Skinner boxes. Maslow's self-actualization thesis is correct: we can and must "invent the future."

According to Theobald, the answer to the future is not destructive revolution but constructive evolution, through such changes as the guaranteed income, the blending of work and leisure, the creation of larger social units than the "nuclear family," and the development of new dwelling patterns suitable for these units (such as modifications of the Navajo "hogan"). We must take the *Whole Earth Catalog* seriously when it says: "We are gods and we might as well get good at it."

The discussion after the lecture predictably elicited a variety of reactions to Theobald's model of the future. Old Testament scholar Harvey Guthrie solemnly asserted that it is legitimate biblically to say "we are gods" (Ps. 82): "the image of God is a role thing." "But how about humility?" a member of the audience asked. This gave Theobald a chance to expand on his theology:

My view of human nature is Chardin's: as man conceives the future so he will become. I don't know the distinction between God and man any more. Where two or three are gathered in the name of cooperation, God is there. We must be *humbler* gods.

Altizer said he was "much disturbed" by Theobald's views. Theobald offers a "new gnosticism," he said, particularly reprehensible because it rejects revolution: "We must have revolution, for the Christian can only choose death, not life." Altizer revised his nineteenth-century revolutionary view of religion, presenting it in even more radical terms than he did during the death-of-God controversy in his book *The Descent Into Hell*. Only by Hegelian dialectic process and Nietzschean eternal recurrence can we "arrive at a new, revolutionary view of consciousness."

The only put-down to the diffuse theologizing of Altizer and of Theobald came—of all places—from the University of Chicago Divinity School's Don Browning. Concerning Altizer:

Don't take him too seriously. The church must not make his mistake of using terms loosely or in the next ten to fifteen years we will lose even more of our credibility.

Of Theobald:

It is good that he rejects the ecological mysticism our church people are falling into, but while we are trying to dig ourselves out a mastery of life motif, he challenges us to develop *new* models of mastery. Religion for him is a vast control device. He may be a good Jew and a good Greek, but he is not a very good Christian.

A small black woman in the audience added the only other word of gospel to appear in the entire session: "You must be born again and not try to do it all yourself." I heard her mutter to herself on the way out: "I can't stand any more of this; I'm going home."

Let us hope that she is not one of the last true Episcopalians. Seabury-Western had ninety theological students ten years ago; today it has sixty, and this decline is reflected throughout the Episcopal seminaries of America. That once noble church has so weakened that it could not even discipline Bishop Pike, who denied the Incarnation and the Trinity; a death-of-God theologian is still considered one of its luminaries; and it can hold a symposium on the future without once mentioning the return of our Lord Jesus Christ to judge the quick and the dead. The Episcopal liturgies remain magnificent, but, to use Pike's famous line, they are sung, not said—regarded aesthetically rather than as affirmations of factual truth.

During the inauguration of Seabury-Western's president, the new incumbent was presented with a Bible and exhorted: "Be among us as one who proclaims the Word." The New Testament lesson was 2 Timothy 3:14–4:5: "The Scriptures are able to make you wise unto salvation through faith in Christ Jesus. All Scripture is given by inspiration of God . . . . Preach the word . . . . The time will come when they will not endure sound doctrine . . . They shall turn away their ears from the truth and shall be turned to myths." Is anybody listening? The future depends on it.

IS THEOLOGY DYING?

Like Pavlov's dog, I predictably salivate when certain stimuli come along. Having been much involved in the death-of-God controversy of the sixties and having written a book called *The Suicide of Christian Theology*, I am the sheer victim of conditioned reflex when an article appears with the title "God Is Not Dead, But Theology Is Dying." My mouth begins immediately to water. Therefore I cannot resist analyzing the thesis embodied in the article of that title that appeared in the December, 1974, issue of *Intellect*—particularly since its author is Charles W. Kegley, coeditor with Robert Bretall of the six-volume Library of Living Theology series, which has given significant scholarly treatment to the thought of Paul Tillich, Reinhold Niebuhr, Emil Brunner, Henry Nelson Wieman, Rudolf Bultmann, and Anders Nygren.

For Kegley, "theology, at least in the Western world, like all Gaul, is divided into three parts," and all are in deep trouble. There is biblical theology, which has classically endeavored to set forth a systematic understanding of the teachings of the Bible; dogmatic theology, interpreting the doctrines of a particular church; and "natural or empirical" theology, illustrated by liberal D. C. Mackintosh's *Theology As an Empirical Science,* which tries to arrive at religious truth without dependence on scriptural revelation.

The first half of the twentieth century, according to Kegley, "appears to have produced the most remarkable collection of brilliant theologians and the most exhaustive systems of theology in the history of Western thought" (he cites the theologians included in his Library of Living Theology series, plus Karl Barth, Nicolaus Berdyaev, and Buddhist Suzuki), but "there not only are no equally creative theologians at work today, there are none on the horizon." Now the biblical theologians are myopically dealing with specialized issues, rather than attempting to understand the sweep of Scripture; the dogmatician, likewise, has given up the great task of comprehending the whole of the faith by way of a "new theological *blick* or stance"; and "as for natural-empirical theology, religious liberalism, like political liberalism just does not excite and sell enough to warrant the writing."

To illustrate this collapse, Kegley zeros in on the "theology of hope" and the more recent "theology of play."

The former illustrates the tendency of the contemporary theologian to "dwarf" his subject matter—to take one (perhaps entirely valid) aspect of the whole and make it everything. "Hope is not any more—and probably is less—likely a candidate than love, faith, or other central concerns of theology" for prime position. In any case the theologian should be offering a synoptic and comprehensive view, not a partial and limited perspective. As for "play theologies," they so distort the broad sweep of biblical religion that they become a "burlesque", a "crude joke." Like today's artist who gives us urinals as works of art, the play theologian (in the double sense) offers "the resurrection of the flesh" (Sam Keen, in *The Theology of Play*, by Moltmann *et al.*).

Why this appalling situation? Kegley cites the American development of the independent theological seminary ("angel factory") separated from the university, and the Supreme Court's Schempp decision in 1963, allowing only "literary" and "historical" study of religion—only talk *about* religion—in secular educational institutions. This decision served to drive the wedge even deeper between so-called objective study of religion and the dedicated work of the theologian, and to move the theologian even farther from the mainstream of intellectual life. And so the understandable tendency today is for the theologian to run away into Transcendence (example: the most recent theologizing of former death-of-god-er Paul Van Buren). Yet "to expound a theology which is incoherent, empirically meaningless, and irrelevant is to misconstrue the task of theology, and to seal its doom *a priori*." What we need is a "theology of God, not of some secular fantasies and games of men," but at the same time a theology which can "so construe its god-talk as to bypass . . . all the criticisms which attach to de-mythologized, literal discussions of God."

Aspects of Kegley's argument can readily be discounted as special pleading: his inclinations toward the "subjective religious empiricism" of early twentieth-century theological modernism cause him to redefine philosophical theology and apologetics as "natural or empirical" theology à la Mackintosh and Wieman. His fascination with his own Library of Living Theology makes him forget Augustine, Aquinas, Luther, Calvin, and others and assert incredibly that theology has now plummeted from the greatest height it ever attained—in the first half of the twentieth century, that is! But apart from Kegley's frustration in not finding a suitable candidate for the seventh volume of his series, he should be listened to carefully.

Theology today *is* superficial and faddish. The important question is, Why? The answer lies much deeper than the separation of theology from religion or the theological seminary from the university (indeed, modern theology's abrogation of its proper task occurred first in the German university faculties of theology in the eighteenth and nineteenth centuries). The central source of the problem—as Kegley himself indirectly suggests in his call for a true "theology of God" and yet a theology that "bypasses" secular criticisms of literal revelation—is that theology is no longer sure of its data. The biblical theologian is unsure to what extent the words and acts of Jesus are the product of primitive belief communities rather than a reflection of Jesus Himself; the systematic theologian, unable to build on such shaky foundations, cannot produce a consistent or comprehensive picture of revelational truth, for no one is sure what is revelation and what is not; and the modern philosophical theologian, having given up special revelation as the source of his operations, has fallen into thinly disguised humanisms devoid of theological substance or appeal (the old modernism, the new "secular theology").

Theology is in the position that medicine would be in if it lost confidence in the germ theory or the use of pharmaceuticals, or law if it found the idea of precedent (*stare decisis*) no longer compelling. Either Scripture speaks univocally of God, or the death of theology is a dead certainty. When will the modern theologian learn that a reliable Bible is his only survival kit?

ENCOUNTER IN FLORENCE

In the spring of 1975, I conducted a seminar-tour to Renaissance Italy. Europe was experiencing its seasonal rebirth; Christendom was celebrating Resurrection victory and Easter newness. Everything conspired to reinforce the impact of that amazing epoch heralding the Reformation which John Addington Symonds referred to as "the fascination of a golden dream." Our regular itinerary gave us Milan's La Scala opera, the Byzantine magnificence of St. Mark's Cathedral in Venice, Petrarch's home at Arqua, the breathtaking Giotto frescoes in Padua, and Florence over the Easter weekend. But an unscheduled theological "extra" was provided in the Renaissance capital: a dialogue of more than routine interest.

It was Easter Monday. On Easter day we had spent time with Riccardo Paul, who is carrying on valiant evangelical missionary work in Florence under the aegis of the Worldwide European Fellowship. Then for two days we had made detailed visits to the Duomo, Ghiberti's golden "doors of paradise" at the Baptistry of San Giovanni, Michelangelo's David at the Accademia delle Belle Arti, Santa Croce, and the house where Christian poets Robert and Elizabeth Barrett Browning lived.

Now, back at our pensione—once a Renaissance palace—we were assembled for one of my lectures. The subject was pre-Reformer Savonarola, who had been burned at the stake on May 23, 1498, and whose ashes had been thrown into the Arno from the Ponte Vecchio. Just before the execution, the bishop declared: "I separate you from the Church Militant and from the Church Triumphant." Replied Savonarola, in words worthy of Luther a generation later: "You may separate me from the Church Militant, but only God can separate me from the Church Triumphant."

As may be evident, I am a Savonarola buff; but I recognize the friar's inadequacies. In my lecture, I quoted his stinging Advent sermon of 1493, in which he condemned the luxury of the Roman church of his day and its indifference to the poor: "The first prelates . . . had fewer gold mitres and fewer chalices, for, indeed, what few they possessed were broken up to relieve the needs of the poor; whereas our prelates, for the sake of obtaining chalices, will rob the poor of their sole means of support." I praised Savonarola for such "law" preaching, but expressed regret that, unlike Luther, he had not been able to provide the positive counteractive: gospel preachment of salvation by grace alone, through faith alone. I emphasized that giving to the poor was no more gospel than giving to the church: a man is saved not by *any thing* he does but by what God has already done for him in Jesus Christ. I noted that one of the greatest sources of weakness in the contemporary church is its confusion of social action with gospel proclamation.

As I spoke I noticed a scholarly fellow in the corner, trying (it appeared) to listen without seeming to listen. He looked like one of that perennial band of sabbatical Fulbright professors in rumpled tweeds studying everything from ancient Roman toilet graffiti to medieval entomology. Who did he turn out to be? A professor of systematic theology from the Garrett Theological Seminary (Evanston, Illinois; United Methodist; pretensions of being evangelical—I well remember my old acquaintance, the English Methodist Luther scholar Philip S. Watson, castigating his colleagues on that faculty for knowing little of Wesley or historic Methodist theology, to say nothing of Luther, whose Romans Commentary brought about Wesley's conversion!). Needless to say, the professor (we'll call him G, for Garrett) had not cared for my lecture. The following dialogue ensued:

G. Giving to the poor is *not* "law."

M. The proper distinction between law and gospel is, as Luther said, the distinguishing mark of the true Christian. We must never confuse justification and sanctification; *all* works are equally inadequate for salvation, no matter how socially beneficial they may be.

G. But works are a *dimension* of the gospel.

M. "Dimension" is a current theological weasel-word; it implies a structural relationship. What structural relationship would permit works to contribute to salvation? Martin Luther King and company are entirely off base when they imply or suggest that serving the poor equals salvation.

G. Such unconscious works *are* saving; don't you think they are done by God's Spirit? Remember what Karl Rahner says about "secret Christians"—those who do God's will though they may not realize it.

M. Like Nebuchadnezzar? Was Pilate saved because the Spirit led him to refuse to take down the superscription from the cross? You are hopelessly confusing *common* grace with *saving* grace.

G. I reject that distinction; there are many good arguments against it.

M. And in behalf of it we have Luther, Calvin, and Scripture.

G. What about giving a cup of water in Jesus' name (Matt. 25)?

M. Do you seriously think the passage means that one not knowing or accepting Christ is in a saving state because he does good from a loving motivation? What about Acts 4:12 (only the name of Jesus saves) and Romans 10:14 (how shall they hear without a preacher)? These passages can only be reconciled by the recognition that Matthew 25 speaks of Christians already saved by grace through faith who haven't yet comprehended how their faith motivates them to do good works—who haven't yet seen good works as the fruit of faith.

G. I don't worry about reconciling Scripture. Do you really think the Bible presents a single, consistent theology?

M. Most definitely, the one Paul (Gal. 1:8) refers to when he says, "Though we, or an angel from heaven [or a professor from Garrett?], preach any other gospel . . . than that which we have preached unto you, let him be accursed."

G. Or a professor from *your* institution?

(Exeunt Omnes.)

Present during my lecture were Pastor Paul and his gracious wife Laura. I thought of them—thirteen years in the barren, heartless, powerfully Communist mission field of Northern Italy. He had told me how hard it was for the two of them and their six children merely to survive the ethical dilemmas (for example, he was told that if he declared more than sixty percent of his income for tax purposes he was crazy, for the government assumes everyone cheats and ups the declared income accordingly!).

His wife explained: "We want people here to see the difference in our lives. Then we can tell them about the Source of our strength and they will listen."

Here were missionaries, like the apostolic company,

whose very lives are predicated on the assumption that "secret Christians" don't exist—that the gospel must be preached in *word*. For them, as for the members of Savonarola's Church Triumphant, God-honoring works are a fruit of faith, never a substitute for it.

ECUMENICITY IN STRASBOURG

One of the very few modern writers who have discussed in English the Protestant religious history of Strasbourg was struck by its antiecumenicity. Franklin L. Ford contrasts the "broad humanity" of the first generation Reformers there (Martin Bucer in particular, who attempted an amalgam of Luther and Calvin) with "the tightlipped orthodoxy" of the Strasbourg religious establishment in the later sixteenth and throughout the seventeenth century: "the population remaining in the city, once the Judentor was closed for the night, was all Christian and overwhelmingly Lutheran" (*Strasbourg in Transition*, Harvard University Press, 1958, p. 18).

But the capital city of the Alsace, on the French-German Rhenish border, was too centrally located to remain uninfluenced by diversity. Today Strasbourg, the seat of the Council of Europe, the Common Market, and the European Court of Human Rights, seems an inevitable choice for ecumenical activity. The Lutheran World Federation (LWF) maintains its Institute for Ecumenical Research there, under the direction of Vilmos Vajta, a transplanted Scandinavian who knows little French but who energetically uses his German and English to promote ecumenical endeavor. Vajta has personally displayed admirable Reformation scholarship; his book *Luther on Worship* is the finest modern treatment of the Reformer's liturgical convictions. But in more recent years he has edited a number of Augsburg and Fortress Press volumes of theological essays whose loose views of the consistency and reliability of Holy Writ would have caused Luther to throw his proverbial inkwell (*The Gospel and Unity; The Gospel and Human Destiny; The Gospel and the Ambiguity of the Church; The Gospel as History*).

In July, 1975, the LWF's Ecumenical Institute brought together some fifty theologians and pastors—from as far as South America, East Germany, Poland, and Czechoslovakia—for its Ninth International Ecumenical Seminar, under the significant but hardly fetching title, "New Transdenominational Movements: Their Ecclesiological and Ecumenical Significance." Normally I would have found it difficult to pry myself loose from the glories of the Alsatian countryside for such a conference, but this one was unique: by "transdenominational movements" Vajta meant the broad theological trends in the present church picture—more especially, the evangelical movement and the social-actionists. Here, finally, was recognition on the continent that evangelical versus nonevangelical belief could be of greater ecumenical significance than ecclesiastical structures and denominational barriers.

The opening essay was devoted expressly to the evangelical position. Gordon Landreth delivered it in his capacity as general secretary of the Evangelical Alliance (London). Inevitably the paper began with personal testimony, but (fortunately) it soon proceeded to set forth a clear and winning statement of what evangelicals stand for: the gospel, the Scriptures, and personal commitment to Christ. "We see ourselves," emphasized Landreth, "as in the line of Augustine, of Luther and Calvin, of Cranmer, Latimer, and Ridley in the English Reformation, of the Puritans, and of Wesley and Whitefield." Landreth noted the impact of evangelical witness both on foreign missions and on social concerns, and reminded his audience of the dynamic influence of Billy Graham, the

Berlin Congress on Evangelism in 1966, and the Congress on World Evangelization in Lausanne (Landreth saw to it that the Lausanne covenant was distributed to each of the participants at Strasbourg).

As a survey of what the evangelical position is, Landreth's paper could not be faulted. Unhappily, as is usually the case in our circles, the essay was essentially a testimony, not a theological justification or an apologia for the evangelical stand. Landreth could not speak as a trained theologian (before serving the Evangelical Alliance he was with the English Inter-Varsity; before that, he was a British Colonial Service officer in Africa); and the result was that his contribution seemed less sophisticated and compelling than it might have been.

Fortunately, other contributors who shared Landreth's biblical perspective were able to supplement his efforts. André Birmelé of the Ecumenical Institute did a superlative critique of "action-centered Christianity"—the secular, political, revolutionary theology that "no longer bases its faith and actions fundamentally in the completed act of salvation by God in the world, but expects salvation as a result of the actions of men, which represent the dead, absent, or non-existent God." Birmelé struck powerfully at the loss of the reality of sin and of any serious Christology in such a viewpoint: "Would it not be more correct to talk simply of 'Jesuology'?" He observed that in action-centered theologians like D. Sölle, the Scriptures are reduced to "giving pointers for building another world": they are demythologized—not on a Heideggerian, existential basis as with Bultmann—but on a Marxist, political, revolutionary model. In this endeavor to "demythologize them from the standpoint of modern history, so that their political intentions can be more clearly set out," biblical reality is "bypassed" and theology "misses its goal."

Johannes Hempel, an East German Lutheran pastor from Dresden, contributed a paper on "The Role and Function of the Ministry in a Changing Church and Society"; it well demonstrated that persecution and difficulty can act as a refiner's fire. Against the backdrop of the lofty biblical conception of the ministry set forth in the Augsburg Confession, Hempel noted "the simply impossible diversity and multiplicity of the pastor's duties today and the expectations made of him." In light of this, the confessions should establish for the pastor "a catalog of priorities," so that he will not waste his ministry on unscriptural goals. "The pastor as the ultimately responsible person (in the parish) is the last man who can exempt himself from his work on behalf of the credibility of the gospel and Christian existence; his personal welfare should come second to this."

At least one of the concluding discussion-group reports betrayed discomfort at the high standard of biblical orthodoxy in an impressive number of the conference contributions. The report rang the changes on the theme which (in my judgment) is the most fundamental fallacy in nonevangelical biblical scholarship and church life: "The New Testament testifies of diverse christologies and diverse types of primitive Christian communities at the heart of the Church itself. . . . The Churches have for their essential mission to offer a place of dialog . . . whereby one can avoid absolutizing the choices." But the absolute need to confess the biblical Christ came through loud and clear at Strasbourg anyway—praise to the One who is the same yesterday, today, and forever!

9

Mass Communication and Scriptural Proclamation*

In a widely used survey of the history of printing, the reader's attention is arrested by this statement: "Islam . . . was uncompromisingly opposed to the reduplication of its sacred writings through the medium of print."[1] Here—in spite of later relaxations of the policy against reproducing the Koran by any technique other than lithography[2]—we have the stark opposition between revealed religion and mass communication: revelation has been given once for all in written form, so to communicate it in any other or more modern way would go against its

---

*Originally delivered as the invitational keynote address at the fourth Verkündiger-Konferenz sponsored by Evangeliums-Rundfunk, the German branch of Trans World Radio, held in Zurich in May 1973.

[1]Douglas C. McMurtrie, *The Book; the Story of Printing and Bookmaking* 3rd rev. ed. (London and New York: Oxford University Press, 1943), p. 93. Cf. Montgomery, "How Muslims Do Apologetics" (ch. 4 of the present work).

[2]See footnote 16 on page 86 of the present work.

sacral character and perhaps constitute an affront to the divine majesty.

Both the man-on-the-street (who may be excused for his ignorance) and a not inconsiderable number of professors of comparative religion (who certainly ought to know better) tell us that "all religions basically teach the same thing." Do all allegedly revealed religions have the same negative view of modern communications? Does the belief in a specific, written Word of God entail by its very nature a suspicion of modern media? Are scriptural proclamation and mass communication by their very nature antithetical concepts?

Whatever may be the case with non-Christian "book religions" or with cults on Christian soil that have supplemented or supplanted the Bible with other sacral writings, I will endeavor to show that the relationship between historic Christianity and mass communication is neither negative nor even neutral; it is of the most positive character. We shall demonstrate, first, that Christianity—not in spite of, but precisely *because of* its focus on scriptural proclamation—places its theological imprimatur upon the communications media and is directly dependent on their services. Secondly, we shall discover that the inherently positive relationship between biblical Christianity and mass communications is like a reversible reaction in chemistry, symbolized by the double-arrow,

$$\longrightarrow$$

$$\longleftarrow$$

for not only does Christianity need the media, but mass communication can only become what it should be when informed by Christian faith. Finally, we shall observe the unique character of biblical proclamation and note the practical implications of this uniqueness for conveying the Christian message by way of the modern media.

CHRISTIANITY NEEDS THE MEDIA

Mass Communications As a Threat?

Christian believers have not always welcomed the modern media with open arms. A mentality not unlike the Moslem opposition to printing has been characteristic of some Christians vis-à-vis technical advances in communications. In the early days of radio, a few voices were raised against the support of religious programming, for such programs were supposed to play into the devil's hands. Was Satan not "the prince of the power of the air"?[3] The desire to correct a later and parallel temptation to reject television wholesale was one of the motivations that led the philosophical apologist Edward John Carnell to step out of his usual role and produce an entire book devoted to the sane analysis of television from the viewpoint of biblical Christianity.[4]

But such negative attitudes on the part of Christian believers toward the modern media were expressed by a very small and almost lunatic fringe, as the tremendous growth of religious radio broadcasting from its beginning in the United States on January 2, 1921, to the present day so eloquently attests.[5] No other religion in the world has so consistently employed the modern media as its servant as has Christianity. One must conclude that those Christians who opposed mass communications reflected not Christian belief *per se* in so doing, but a personal conser-

---

[3]T.C. Horton alluded to this bizarre exegesis of Ephesians 2:2 in a short note, "Restless over the Radio," in *The King's Business*, Vol. 14 /No. 9 (September, 1923), p. 901.

[4]Edward John Carnell, *Television: Servant or Master?* (Grand Rapids, Michigan: Eerdmans, 1950).

[5]This date marks the beginning of the history of religious broadcasting. Edwin Van Etten, rector of Calvary Episcopal Church of Pittsburgh, Pa., conducted an Epiphany service over Pittsburgh station KDKA.

vatism of temperament that had little to do with their Christianity, just as the political rightism of some Christians today operates independently of and often in direct tension with biblical principles.[6]

Perhaps, however, there is a matter of Christian principle involved in the reticence of some believers to embrace the modern media. Does not a proper biblical posture of separation from this world justify such an attitude? Is not Satan the "god of this world" and do not the technological advances of modern pagan civilization reflect the fallen Prometheus who defies the gods, and the makers of the tower of Babel who seek to reach heaven through their own accomplishments? In this light, does not the designation of Satan as the "prince of the power of the air" relate more seriously to modern communications than one might suppose at first glance? Should not our separation from evil dictate also our separation from communication techniques unrelated to the personal encounters by which men came to Jesus in New Testament times?

Here we meet one of the most persistent and dangerous undertows in the river of salvation: not a current, only an undertow, in the history of Christian thought, but fully capable of drowning its victims. The fundamental error of this pietism—which has as its motto the phrase of the Anglican littérateur Charles Williams, "neither is this Thou"—is its abrogation of the world to the devil. Nothing in the world is regarded as actually, or even potentially, sacramental. The pietist is tricked by Satan's lie to Jesus when he tempted our Lord in the wilderness: "The devil, taking him up into an high mountain, showed unto him all the kingdoms of the world in a moment of time. And the devil said unto him, All this power will I give thee,

---

[6]Cf. Richard V. Pierard, *The Unequal Yoke: Evangelical Christianity and Political Conservatism* ("Evangelical Perspectives," ed. John Warwick Montgomery; Philadelphia: J.B. Lippincott, 1970).

and the glory of them: for that is delivered unto me; and to whomsoever I will I give it" (Luke 4: 5, 6). In point of fact, the kingdoms of the world were not Satan's to give. They remained entirely in God's hands, and were thus Christ's already. Thus Jesus quite properly replied to the devil's offer with the authoritative word of Scripture: "Thou shalt worship the Lord thy God, and him only shalt thou serve" (Luke 4:8, quoting Deut. 6:13; 10:20). On another occasion, Jesus said expressly that the devil "abode not in the truth, because there is no truth in him. When he speaketh a lie, he speaketh of his own: for he is a liar, and the father of it" (John 8:44). The pietist takes Satan too seriously when he claims to control the world; he should recognize, as the Book of Job so clearly teaches, that the Evil One operates on a stringently controlled scale, within the strict framework of God's sovereign will.[7]

This is how the classic commentators have understood the phrase, κατὰ τὸν ἄρχοντα τῆσ εξουσίας τοῦ ἀέρος, in Ephesians 2:2. The great dogmatician and exegete of the period of high Lutheran orthodoxy, Abraham Calov (1612–1686), notes in his *Biblia Novi Testamenti illustrate* that the passage does not mean, as Theodoret thought, that Satan had originally been created as governor of the region of the air, but rather, as Theophylact perceived: "Paul calls him the prince of the power of the air, not because he has any sovereignty over the air, as for example in ruling or regulating it, but—far from it—because he has surreptitiously entered into that region."[8] J. A. Bengel rightly observed in his *Gnomon* that the Pauline ex-

---

[7]See Montgomery, *Principalities and Powers: The World of the Occult* (Minneapolis: Bethany, 1973), especially ch. 6 ("God's Devil"), pp. 151–66.

[8]*Et ideo Paulus Principem potestatis aeris dicit, non quod ullam habeat in aere ditionem, ut illum scil. vel temperet vel moderetur, id quidem sit procul, sed quia se in illo insinuet* (Abraham Calov, *Biblia Novi Testamenti illustrata* (2 vols.; Dresden & Leipzig: J. C. Zimmermann, 1719), II, 672).

pression means that *"haec potestas est late diffusa et penetrans"* (Satan's power is widely diffused and penetrating), and cautioned his pietistic readers that *"Christus tamen superior est Satana, quamvis etiam in* ἐπουρανίοις *se hic teneat"* (Christ is superior to Satan, even though the latter also abides in heavenly places).[9] As a parallel passage, Bengel appropriately cites the opening chapter of Job.

Those Christians who have separated themselves from mass communications have in reality done so not on the basis of scriptural principle but in reaction to unbelievers or rationalistic churchmen who have made a god of the media or turned the media to doubtful purposes. But, ironically, such a solution to a very real problem only compounds the evil, for it gives a powerful tool entirely into the hands of the wrong users. Moreover, it pulls the believing Christian down to the level of the unbeliever or inconsistent churchman, for the latter has erred in allowing the *Zeitgeist,* not Scripture, to create and condition his theology and practice. The believer, then, by developing a theology in reaction against this extreme instead of on the basis of what the Bible says, finds himself also mirroring the human situation, for his views are rigidly molded by what he is reacting against. This is an exact parallel to the unbiblical fundamentalistic reaction against social amelioration, created by a desire to oppose the liberal "social gospel" and exceeding the desire to be faithful to Holy Scripture.[10]

The confessing Christian believer rightly opposes—in theory—the basic operative motif of Bultmannian and

[9]J.A. Bengel, *Gnomon Novi Testamenti* 3rd ed., 1773 rev. (Stuttgart: J.F. Steinkopf, 1866), p. 746.

[10]Cf. David O. Moberg, *The Great Reversal: Evangelism versus Social Concern* ("Evangelical Perspectives," ed. John Warwick Montgomery; Philadelphia: J.B. Lippincott, 1972).

post-Bultmannian theology: the "hermeneutical circle." This conception finds an existential "life relation" subsisting between the biblical text and the interpreter, and the result is a necessary circularity in all scriptural interpretation (the interpreter influences the text even as the text influences the interpreter), and no exegesis can ever be regarded as genuinely objective.[11] As Ernst Käsemann puts it, following in his master's (Bultmann's) footsteps: "The Word, as biblical criticism makes plain, has no existence in the realm of the objective—that is, outside our act of decision."[12] Christians in the historic, confessional tradition rightly see that such an approach substitutes for God's objective proclamation to man a relativistic confusion of God's truth and man's sinful situation, with no possibility of distinguishing the two. Man loses all possibility of a clear word of salvation, and the dog returns to his own existential vomit. But let us carry out the implications of our criticism of Bultmannianism in practice: let us not determine our attitude toward mass communication by reacting against non-Christian attitudes (for this is simply to enter a new hermeneutical circle), but let us allow Scripture alone to dictate the approach that we should take to these remarkable modern media. If we do, we shall quickly discover that mass communication, far from being a threat to scriptural proclamation, relates to its central teachings in the most positive way.

---

[11]See especially Rudolf Bultmann, "Ist voraussetzungslose Exegese möglich?," *Theologische Zeitschrift*, Vol. 13 (1957), pp. 409–17.

[12]Ernst Käsemann, *Exegetische Versuche und Besinnungen*, Vol. 1, 2nd ed. (Göttingen: Vandenhoeck & Ruprecht, 1960), pp. 232–33. In critique: Montgomery, *Crisis in Lutheran Theology*, 2 vols., rev. ed. (Minneapolis: Bethany, 1973), Vol. 1, pp. 45–77. (For the German version of this essay, see "Lutherische Hermeneutik-und Hermeneutik Heute," *Lutherischer Rundblick*, Vol. 15, No. 1 [I. Quartal, 1967] pp. 2–32).

The Trinity and Eternal Communication

Nothing could be more basic to historic, confessional Christianity than the doctrines of the Trinitarian nature of Deity and Christ as the incarnate Word of God. The three ecumenical creeds of Christendom—the Apostles' Creed, the Nicene Creed, and the Athanasian Creed—which constitute the defining mark of all confessional Christians, whether Eastern Orthodox, Roman Catholic, or Protestant, focus directly upon these doctrines. The early church rightly recognized that Trinity and Logos are at the very heart of biblical teaching.[13]

Much less commonly recognized, however, are the implications of these fundamental doctrines for a Christian philosophy of communications. In point of fact, both the Trinitarian understanding of God and the conception of the Second Person of the Trinity as Logos bind the very idea of communication into the heart of Christian faith. Consider first the Trinity.

What was God doing before the creation of the world? Luther enjoyed Augustine's suggestion in his *Confessions* that God may have been making hell ready for those who pried into such meddlesome questions![14] Certainly non-Christian religions, with unitarian views of God, can say nothing whatever in answer to such a question, and Luther was striking out against those religionists who preferred to speculate on the basis of an anthropocentric *theologia gloriae crucis*.[15] But Christianity can, on the

---

[13]On the derivation of Trinitarian doctrine from the Bible and its parallel with scientific inference, see Montgomery, "The Theologian's Craft: A Discussion of Theory Formation and Theory Testing in Theology," *Suicide of Christian Theology* (Minneapolis: Bethany, 1970), pp. 267–313, especially pp. 297–99.

[14]WA, Vol. 42, No. 9 (commentary on Gen. 1: 2 [1535]). Augustine (*Confessions*, Bk. 9) considers this facetious answer to "elude the pressure of the question" and uses it as his entree into a discussion of the nature of Time.

[15]Cf. Paul Althaus, *Die Theologie Martin Luthers*, 2nd ed. (Gütersloh: Gütersloher Verlagshaus Gerd Mohn, 1963), Sec. 5.

basis of scriptural revelation, say at least one thing about God in eternity, prior to the creation: He was a God of love even before the foundation of the world. How is this possible, since love cannot exist in isolation, but requires communication between at least two persons? The Christian alone can answer confidently: because God has been from eternity three Persons in one Godhead, and the mutual love of Father, Son, and Holy Spirit has been communicated eternally. When Aristotle conceived of his unitary Prime Mover as contemplative "thought thinking on itself"—spending eternity loving itself, since there was nothing higher to love—he necessarily defined love in terms of self-centered ῎Ερως, which is not love at all but a kind of cosmic narcissism.[16]

Among the world's religions and philosophies, only a Trinitarian conception of God offers the genuine possibility of conceiving God as self-giving love by His very nature, even before the world came into existence as a focus for that love. As James Orr so well expressed it in his classic, *The Christian View of God and the World:* "If, therefore, God is love in Himself—in His own eternal and transcendent being—He must have in some way within Himself the perfect and eternal object of His love—which is just the Scripture doctrine of the Son. This view of God is completed in the perfect communion the Divine Persons have with each other through the Holy Spirit—the bond and medium of their love."[17]

The perfect communion and communication within the Godhead from eternity removes all need to move in the heretical direction of today's "process theology" in order to arrive at a meaningful view of God's personality. The

---

[16] Aristotle, *Metaphysics*, Bk. Λ, 1072b. Cf. Anders Nygren's classic treatment of the subject in his *Agape and Eros*, E.T. (London: SPCK, 1953).

[17] James Orr, *The Christian View of God and the World, As Centering in the Incarnation*, 3rd ed. (Edinburgh: Andrew Elliot, 1897), p. 274.

process theologians, such as Norman Pittenger, Schubert Ogden, and John B. Cobb, Jr., reflecting the current man-centered and secular trend of Protestant thought, derive from the panentheism of Hartshorne and the metaphysics of Whitehead a concept of God who is in some sense dependent on or in phase with His creation; He grows, develops, evolves in the mutuality of His relations with His creatures.[18] But as Manchester exegete A. S. Peake observed over a half-century ago, such theologizing creates more problems than it solves, and any philosophical advantages it may seem to possess are vastly inferior to those of biblical Trinitarianism:

> We achieve a sense of our own personality only in the society of our fellows. We can win it to a certain extent by contrast with animate and inanimate nature, but the deepest elements of our personality can find their satisfaction only in those who are constituted as ourselves. And, similarly, the material universe could never suffice for the need of the Creator. But neither can we make God dependent for self-realisation on personalities outside Himself. This woul' mean that God could not be completely God till He had created spirits for fellowship with Himself, and so once again His absoluteness would be impaired and the Infinite made to depend on the finite for His perfection. Thus the doctrine of the Trinity guards the personality of God. . . . The postulates, that self-consciousness depends for its existence on a society, that the self can know itself only through contrast with the not-self, and, further, that love necessitates the lover and the loved, find their satisfaction in the Christian conception of God as no bare and abstract unity, but a unity rich and complex, embracing different centres of consciousness in mutual relation.[19]

---

[18]See inter alia, John B. Cobb, Jr., *A Christian Natural Theology* (Philadelphia: Westminster, 1965); Norman Pittenger, *Process-Thought and Christian Faith* (New York: Macmillan, 1968); and—as general philosophical background—William A. Christian, *An Interpretation of Whitehead's Metaphysics* (New Haven, Conn.: Yale University Press, 1959).

[19]Arthur S. Peake, *Christianity: Its Nature and Its Truth*, 10th ed. (London: Duckworth, 1915), pp. 100–103.

The God of the Bible has always been "in society" and "in mutual relation" and has therefore always been Communicator. When Christians encounter the field of communications, they do not enter an alien territory. Their God, by His *very nature*, has always been there; indeed, the very field of communication is in a most literal sense a reflection of the very being of the Trinitarian Deity of biblical religion.

The Logos and Temporal Communication

When scriptural revelation casts its spotlight from eternity to time, the concept of God as Communicator is even more sharply illuminated. The Second Person of the Holy Trinity is designated the Logos—the Word, the self-communication of the eternal God—and it is He who becomes flesh (John 1: 1,14). The Triune God, out of love, deigns to communicate with the fallen race and does so by the incarnation of the eternal Word, who conveys God's message to those dead in trespasses and sins: "Never man spake like this man" (John 7:46).

The church in its earliest history settled the question of the reality of this divine communication. It rejected all forms of docetism—the heretical notion that the Logos only "seemed" (Gr. δοκεῖν) to become a man. Thus Ignatius of Antioch, on his way to martyrdom under the Emperor Trajan (A.D. 107), wrote that Christ "truly suffered even as also He truly raised Himself up, not as some faithless persons say, that His passion was a matter of semblance, whereas it is they who are mere semblance. Things will assuredly turn out for them in accord with their opinions: they will find themselves disembodied and phantasmal."[20] We today should make equally certain that we do not create a "disembodied and phantasmal" theology by accepting Martin Kähler's distinction be-

---

[20]Ignatius of Antioch, *To the Smyrnaeans*, p. ii.

tween the "ordinary," that is, nonmiraculous, events
recorded in Scripture *(Historie)* and the allegedly "suprahistorical" or "metahistorical" events of miraculous,
incarnational, salvatory history *(Heilsgeschichte)*.[21] This
historical dualism, which has so deeply influenced Barthian theology, is dangerous in the extreme, for it places the
Incarnation in a realm beyond meaningful historical
analysis, and therefore (by definition) beyond genuine
history itself.[22] Wolfhart Pannenberg, notwithstanding
his grossly deficient conception of biblical inspiration, has
performed a great service in unqualifiedly opposing the
Historie-Geschichte dichotomy and insisting on a truly
historical understanding of the saving events of the Incarnation.[23] The Word entered our historical framework in
the most literal sense, and thus specifically hallowed the
use of human communication in imparting divine truth.

This concrete parallel can readily be seen on the basis of
a diagram of the human communication system developed
by one of the foremost communications theorists of our
day, Professor Wilbur Schramm, Aw Boon Haw Professor of Communications at the Chinese University of Hong
Kong:

---

[21]Cf. the title of Kähler's most influential work: *Der sogenannte historische
Jesus and der geschichtliche, biblische Christus* (München: Chr. Kaiser Verlag,
1956 [1st ed., 1892]), E.T. *The So-called historical Jesus and the historic,
biblical Christ* (Philadelphia: Fortress Press, 1964).

[22]See Montgomery, "Karl Barth and Contemporary Theology of History,"
Where Is History Going? reprint ed. (Minneapolis: Bethany, 1972), pp. 100–17.
(This work will shortly appear in a German version published by Hänssler-
Verlag in Neuhausen-Stuttgart.)

[23]Pannenberg's two major publications are *Offenbarung als Geschichte* (the 2nd
ed. of 1963 contains a significant appendix in which the author criticizes his
critics) and *Grundzuge der Christologie* (1964). For an exceedingly valuable
treatment of the genuine historicity of the Incarnation, see Oscar Cullmann,
Heil als Geschichte (Tübingen: J.C.B. Mohr [Paul Siebeck], 1965), E.T. *Salvation in History* (London: S.C.M., 1967).

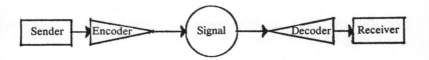

Comments Schramm: "Substitute 'microphone' for 'encoder', and 'earphone' for 'decoder,' and you are talking about electronic communication. Consider that the 'sender' and 'encoder' are one person, 'decoder' and 'receiver' are another, and the signal is language, and you are talking about human communication."[24] But note that this fundamental communications diagram serves equally well as a schematic model of the Incarnation! The "signal" is the Logos—the Word of God—in its primary sense as the Second Person of the Trinity, conveying God's message to man, the receiver, from the eternal Sender, but also in its secondary and derived senses of the gospel (the message of Christ) and the Holy Scriptures (which are able to make us "wise unto salvation through faith which is in Christ Jesus—see 2 Timothy 3:15–17). Here we see with utter clarity how the very plan of salvation is a communications enterprise, and perhaps we begin to appreciate what a powerful stake Christianity has in the realm of the media.

That the parallel we are drawing is by no means artificial becomes even more obvious (if possible) when we consider the four "proper conditions for communication" which Schramm induces from the above schematic formulation:

[24]Wilbur Schramm, "Procedures and Effects of Mass Communication," in *Mass Media and Education: The 53rd Yearbook of the National Society for the Study of Education, Part II*, ed. Nelson B. Henry (Chicago: University of Chicago Press, 1954), pp. 114–15.

(1) The message must be so designed and delivered as to gain the attention of the intended receiver.

(2) The message must employ signs which refer to experience common to both sender and receiver, so as to "get the meaning across."

(3) The message must arouse personality needs in the receiver and suggest some ways to meet those needs.

(4) The message must suggest a way to meet those needs which is appropriate to the group situation in which the receiver finds himself at the time when he is moved to make the desired response.[25]

If we now contemplate God's perfect communication of Himself to us in the incarnation of Christ, we see how fully these principles apply to it. First, God "gained our attention" by a prophetic preparation for the coming of the Messiah which extended from the Protoevangelion in Genesis 3:15 to the last words of the Old Testament, and by the miraculous life of Christ on earth which commenced in a virgin birth and ended with the Resurrection and Ascension into heaven.

Next, the salvation God provided employed the sign of the Cross—extending from heaven to earth—to "refer to experience common to both sender and receiver." The Savior linked heaven and earth, for He was fully God, yet fully man—"in all points tempted like as we are, yet without sin" (Heb. 4:15). Thus could He die in our stead, for He was our Brother, the Second Adam.

Third, God's message in Christ aroused our most basic "personality need": the need to be reconciled to God. When faced with His demand for perfection, as set forth in the Sermon on the Mount (Matt. 5:48) and as exemplified

---

[25]*Ibid.*, p. 121.

in His own spotless life, men dropped to their knees and cried, "Depart from me, for I am a sinful man, O Lord" (Luke 5:8), thus opening the way for Him to pick them up and restore them to perfect fellowship with God.

Finally the saving message of Christ never left men in doubt as to how their needs could be met: not by works, but by the faith that accepts Christ as the only Savior. "Then said they unto him, What shall we do, that we might work the works of God? Jesus answered and said unto them, This is the work of God, that ye believe on him whom he hath sent" (John 6: 28, 29). The "group situation" in which man found—and finds—himself when encountered by the incarnate Christ is one strewn with the debris of towers of Babel which man has unsuccessfully raised to gain heaven by his own efforts. The Incarnation offers the only remedy for this: "No man hath ascended up to heaven, but He that came down from heaven, even the Son of man. . ." (John 3:13).

The Fullness of Time

We could likewise show, with no difficulty whatever, that the scriptural principles for proclaiming the incarnational gospel to others entail these very same "proper conditions for communication"—an especially telling example being the comparison between the second condition ("common experience") and the Pauline axiom that in order to bring men to a saving knowledge of Christ, the Apostle became "all things to all men" (1 Cor. 9:22).[26] Indeed, an analysis of what C. H. Dodd termed "the Apostolic preaching and its developments"—the sermons in the Book of Acts—in terms of these conditions for

---

[26]See the excellent discussion of this key Pauline theme in Richard N. Longenecker's *Paul, Apostle of Liberty* (New York: Harper, 1964), ch. 10, pp. 230–44.

successful communication would demonstrate how fully the imparting of the Divine Word is a communicative act.

But a less obvious parallel between scriptural proclamation and mass communication warrants our attention, for it will help to put the great truth of the inherently communicative nature of the Christian faith into full historical perspective. We are all familiar with Paul's assertion in Galatians 4:4 that God sent forth His Son "when the fulness of the time was come." But in what sense exactly did the Advent of our Lord occur at τὸ πλήρωμα τοῦ χρόνου? The prophetic times were fulfilled, to be sure;[27] but a neglected work by a contemporary English classical scholar allows us to hypothesize that equally important may have been the evolution of communications in the secular world of the first century! Lawrence Waddy, in his valuable book, *Pax Romana and World Peace,* shows that conditions at the time of Christ's coming were ideal for the rapid dissemination of God's Word. His discussion, explanatory table, and map warrant reproduction here:

> The great material achievement of the Romans was the making of their communications. The map here inset is designed to show some of the main roads and shipping routes, and the times recorded as having been taken by travellers over different journeys. These times were sometimes quoted because they had been exceptionally fast, but they may be allowed to give a fair picture of what was possible for the ordinary traveller. They compare favourably with anything to be found in accounts of travel in France or England before the Industrial Revolution. A Roman traveller went faster, on the whole, than the characters in a Jane Austen novel. He did not meet turnpikes, nor as a rule roads full of pot-holes. . . . Strange results occur if we try to transpose (St. Paul's) journeys into a modern

---

[27]See especially Sir Robert Anderson, *The Coming Prince,* 11th ed. (Glasgow: Pickering & Inglis, n.d.); and cf. Montgomery, *Principalities and Powers,* pp. 121–29.

context. Paul and his companions "loosed from Paphos, and came to Perga in Pamphylia," we read. Paphos is in British Cyprus, Perga on the south coast of Turkey. Paul was a Greek-speaking Jew from Turkey, but a Roman citizen, and his travelling companion Barnabas was a Cypriote. They simply went down to the harbour at Paphos and booked a passage. Could you and I do the same, without a great deal of questioning and form-filling? Read chapters 16 and 17 of the Acts of the Apostles with a modern atlas in front of you. A map of Italy, the Balkans and Turkey in Bartholomew's *Comparative Atlas* marks in the political frontiers, and adds in the corner an "ethnographic sketch map." St. Paul was familiar with Greek terms, and would have understood the meaning of the word "ethnographic"; but he would have been at a loss to know what the map was all about. The area through which he made his journeys would certainly be a thorny one to the modern traveller. How much delay and difficulty would there be in obtaining permits, passports, visas, supplies of currency and so on, before one could pass between Bulgaria, Yugoslavia and Greece, to name only three of the countries through which he journeyed? Yet from the time of Augustus a good road ran from Durazzo (Dyrracchium) and Valona (Apollonia) in Albania, through the mountain passes of Yugoslavia to Salonica, and on to Istanbul; and for most of the way it lay in the Roman province of Macedonia, in which no regular troops were stationed at all. Is this contrast unfair? There are admittedly large areas in the modern world where no passport is needed: the United States, Australia, and until recently India. But these are only separate compartments in our expanded world of seventy sovereign states. Rome virtually was the civilized world.

All roads led to Rome in Augustus' Empire.[28]

[28]Lawrence Waddy, *Pax Romana and World Peace* (London: Chapman and Hall Limited, n.d.), pp. 122–23. I had the privilege of personal contact with Anglican Father Waddy, now with the English Department of the University of California at San Diego, while I was attached to the University's Department of Philosophy as Honorary Fellow of Revelle College during the winter quarter of the 1969–70 academic year. (The situation has not improved since Fr. Waddy wrote. Cyprus is now more divided than ever it was under British rule, and the number of independent sovereign states in the world has increased rapidly.— Ed. of *The Evangelical Quarterly*)

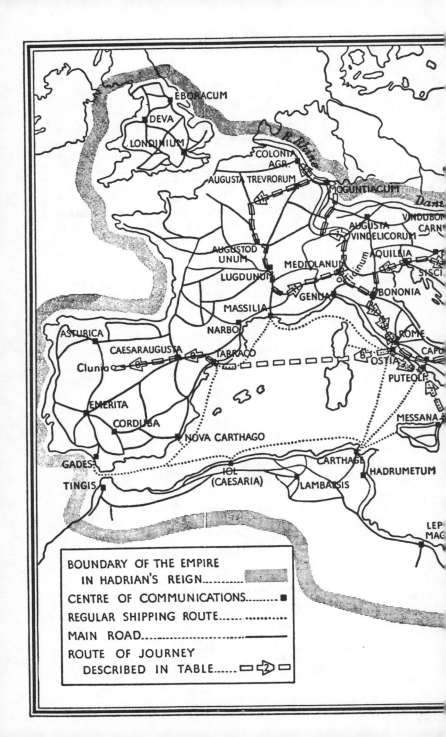

BOUNDARY OF THE EMPIRE
IN HADRIAN'S REIGN............
CENTRE OF COMMUNICATIONS..........■
REGULAR SHIPPING ROUTE.................
MAIN ROAD........................
ROUTE OF JOURNEY
DESCRIBED IN TABLE......◻⇨◻

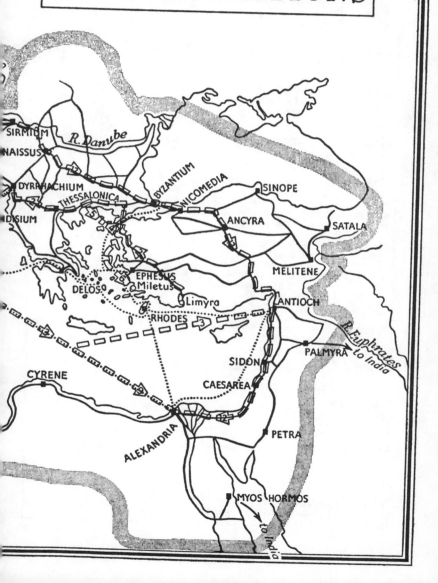

ROMAN COMMUNICATIONS

EXPLANATORY TABLE

(The routes shown are partly conjectural)

	Date	Details of Journey (Approx. Dist. in Eng. miles)	Average Speed For How Long	Facilities	Reference
1	9 B.C.	Tiberius:180 miles in 1 day	180 for 1 day	Exceptional	Valerius Maximus, *Facta Memorabilia,* v, 3
2	A.D. 4	Special Messenger: Lycia-Rome: 1300+ miles in ?36 days	45-50 for 36 days	Exceptional	Inscription (D. 140)
3	A.D. 41	Imperial Courier: Rome-Antioch by sea, bad weather: 3 months	-	-	Josephus, *Bell. Jud.* ii, 10,5
4	?A.D. 49	St. Paul: Troas-Neapolis (port near Philippi): 140 miles by sea in 2 days	70 for 2 days	-	Acts xvi, 11
5	?A.D. 56	St. Paul: Philippi-Troas: by sea, 5 days	30 for 5 days	-	Acts xx, 6
6	?A.D. 56	St. Paul: Mitylene-Miletus: by sea, 3 days	-	-	Acts xx, 15
7	?A.D. 62	St. Paul: Rhegium-Puteoli: by sea, 1 day	200 for 1 day	-	Acts xxviii, 14
8	A.D. 68	Special Messenger: Rome-Clunia, ?6½ days (including Tarraco-Clunia, 332 miles in ?1½ days)	190 for 1½ days	Exceptional	Plutarch, *Galba* 7
9	A.D. 68	Imperial Courier: Rome-Alexandria by sea, 28 days or less	-	-	Inscription
10	A.D. 69	Special Messenger: Mainz-Cologne: 100 miles in ?12 hours	200 for ½ day	Exceptional	Tac. *Hist.* i, 56
11	A.D. 69	Special Messenger: Mainz-Rheims-Rome: 1300+ miles in ?9 days	145 for 9 days	Exceptional	Tac. *Hist.* i, 12
12	A.D. 193	Imperial Courier: Rome-Alexandria: by land, distance uncertain, 63–64 days	-	Exceptional	Inscription
13	A.D. 238	Imperial Courier: Aquileia-Rome: 470 miles in 3-4 days	120 for 4 days	Exceptional	S.H.A. *Duo Max.* 25

Not only physical, but also linguistic communication had attained a πλήρωμα at the time the Word became flesh. Alexander's conquests had brought the Greek tongue, in the form today known as the κοινή, to the level of a world-speech which served in the first century A.D. as the language of the New Testament and the vehicle for the universal spread of the gospel. Following Wilamowitz-Möllendorff, A. T. Robertson writes in his monumental *Grammar of the Greek New Testament in the Light of Historical Research:*

> It is not speculation to speak of the κοινή as a world-speech, for the inscriptions in the κοινή testify to its spread over Asia, Egypt, Greece, Italy, Sicily and the isles of the sea, not to mention the papyri. Marseilles was a great centre of Greek civilization, and even Cyrene, though not Carthage, was Grecized. The κοινή was in such general use that the Roman Senate and imperial governors had the decrees translated into the world-language and scattered over the empire. It is significant that the Greek speech becomes one instead of many dialects at the very time that the Roman rule sweeps over the world. The language spread by Alexander's army over the Eastern world persisted after the division of the kingdom and penetrated all parts of the Roman world, even Rome itself. Paul wrote to the church at Rome in Greek, and Marcus Aurelius, the Roman Emperor, wrote his *Meditations* (τῶν εἰς ‘Εαυτόν) in Greek. It was the language not only of letters, but of commerce and every-day life. . . . It was really an epoch in the world's history when the babel of tongues was hushed in the wonderful language of Geece.[29]

Another master philologist, James Hope Moulton, well summarized the double impact of this linguistic and physical communications-revolution which served as

---

[29] A.T. Robertson, *A Grammar of the Greek New Testament in the Light of Historical Research,* 4th ed. (London: Hodder & Stoughton; New York: George H. Doran, 1923), pp. 54–55.

praeparatio evangelii; note his wryly effective introduction of teleology into the discussion:

> No one can fail to see how immeasurably important these conditions were for the growth of Christianity. The historian marks the fact that the Gospel began its career of conquest at the one period in the world's annals when civilisation was concentrated under a single ruler. The grammarian adds that this was the only period when a single language was understood throughout the countries which counted for the history of that Empire. The historian and the grammarian must of course refrain from talking about "Providence." They would be suspected of "an apologetic bias" or "an edifying tone," and that is necessarily fatal to any reputation for scientific attainment. We will only remark that some old-fashioned people are disposed to see in these facts a σημεῖον in its way as instructive as the Gift of Tongues.[30]

Thus we have every reason to believe that communications factors such as the Roman road system and a universal language were directly bound up with the "fulness of time" for the impartation of the gospel. This seems only natural when we recall the eternal Trinitarian communicativeness and the designation of the Savior as God's Word to man. Now, moreover, we have acquired a principle of historical analysis which is of inestimable value in examining the spread of the gospel through the ages. Just as communications media were vital to the original proclamation of the gospel in Christ's coming, so they have served as fundamental to the recovery and dissemination of that same World in later times.

Consider the success of the Protestant Reformation. "Above all," declares Frederic Seebohm, author of the perennial classic, *The Oxford Reformers,* "the invention of printing had come just in time to spread whatever new

---

[30]James Hope Moulton, *A Grammar of New Testament Greek,* Vol. 1, 3rd rev. ed. (Edinburgh: T&T Clark, 1908), p. 6.

ideas were afloat with a rapidity never before known."[31]
Echoes Harold J. Grimm: "The importance of printing in
the spread of the Reformation can scarcely be exagger-
ated."[32] G. R. Elton makes the not implausible suggestion
that "Luther might have been only another Wycliffe . . . if
the printing press had not given him the chance of appealing to favourable sentiments far and wide."[33] No one who
has visited the permanent exhibit of "Der Buchdruck im
16. Jahrhundert" at the Gutenberg Museum in Mainz can
doubt the truth of these observations.[34] From the standpoint of bibliographical history, Denys Hay summarizes
the evidence in the following terms:

> The vast quantities of pamphlets issued in Germany (630
> have been listed from the years 1520 to 1530) leave no doubt
> that without the printing press the course of the German
> Reformation might have been different. Luther's own writ-
> ings constitute a third of the German books printed in the
> first four decades of the sixteenth century; his address *To
> the Christian Nobility of the German Nation* (August 1520)
> was reprinted thirteen times in two years; *Concerning
> Christian Liberty* (September 1520) came out eighteen
> times before 1526; as for his translation of the Bible, Dr.
> Steinberg summarizes the complicated bibliographical
> story thus—"All in all, 430 editions of the whole Bible or
> parts of it appeared during Luther's lifetime."[35]

[31]Frederic Seebohm, *The Era of the Protestant Revolution*, 2nd ed. (New York: Scribner, 1893), p. 4.

[32]Harold J. Grimm, *The Reformation Era: 1500–1650* (New York: Macmillan, 1954), p. 160.

[33]*The New Cambridge Modern History*, Vol. 2: *The Reformation, 1520–1559*, ed. G.R. Elton (Cambridge, Eng.: Cambridge University Press, 1958), p. 17.

[34]Display cases 140–150. Cf. Helmut Presser, *Gutenberg-Museum der Stadt Mainz: Weltmuseum der Druckkunst* 2nd ed. (München: Peter-Winkler-Verlag, 1966), pp. 38–39.

[35]Denys Hay, "Fiat Lux," in *Printing and the Mind of Man: A Descriptive Catalogue Illustrating the Impact of Print on the Evolution of Western Civiliza-tion*, ed. John Carter and Percy H. Muir (London: Cassell, 1967), p. xxix and see catalog entries 49–51, 56, 58, 65). Cf. A. Kuczynski, *Verzeichnis einer Sammlung von nahezu 3000 Flugschriften Luthers und seiner Zeitgenossen* (Leipzig, 1870).

Must we not say that the eternal Logos employed the mass communication technique of printing to insure and further the recovery of His gospel in the sixteenth century, even as He used Roman communications and the Greek language in the original dissemination of it in the first century? Would not the apostles have sinned terribly had they refused to use the Roman roads because they were the product of a heathen and materialistic civilization or the Greek tongue because it was the vehicle of pagan philosophy? Would not the Reformers have denied their calling if they had pietistically rejected the printing press as a technique already employed for making playing cards, issuing indulgences, and disseminating the literature of non-Christian antiquity? Fortunately—for them and for us—they recognized that the God of Christianity is uniquely a communicative Deity and that techniques of communication are not to be given over to the devil and his minions, but are to be employed for the glory of the One whose nature they reflect.

Perhaps we regard as fanciful the mass communications interpretation of Relevation 1:7 ("Behold, he cometh with clouds; and every eye shall see him, and they also which pierced him: and all kindreds of the earth shall wail because of him") which contends that only with the invention of television in our own generation has this ubiquitous seeing become technically possible. But, fanciful or not, the interpretation recognizes the great theological truth that the Christian God incorporates the techniques of mass communication into His sovereign plan for the ages. He expects believers in every age to cultivate a sensitive awareness of the media possibilities uniquely open to them for imparting the eternal riches of His grace to their particular generation. Are we personally carrying out this commission to the maximum?

THE MEDIA NEED CHRISTIANITY

A secular media man could well have followed our discussion to this point and—descriptively at least—agreed with it: the Christian religion is uniquely and inherently favorable to communication and must, to be consistent with its God and its gospel, involve itself in mass communication technique. But when we turn to the other side of the coin—the contribution of the Christian message to the media—the reaction may well be, "Like who needs it, man?"

Answer: *You* do, secular communicator, and *desperately*.

In a sense, to be sure, the foregoing discussion has already indicated that the relationship between scriptural proclamation and mass communication is a two-way street, for if God is indeed the Trinitarian Deity the Bible says He is, and if He did manifest Himself as the Word made flesh, then all communication has its existence and possibility only in Him. Just as human creative activity necessarily reflects the Creator of all,[36] so human communication is essentially and by its very nature a reflection of the communicative God. Conversely, to the extent that one separates himself from the eternal Word, to that degree he loses his ability truly to communicate. But these fundamental truths need to be driven home in the context of the present-day cacophony in mass communications.

The noise level in modern life is becoming almost unbearable. In terms of literal decibels the problem is serious enough, but it by no means stops there. Radio and television announcers, whatever their language or country, develop a truly remarkable capacity for facile speech which allows them to talk incessantly in a manner suggesting

---

[36]Cf. Dorothy L. Sayers, *The Mind of the Maker* (New York: Meridian Living Age Books, 1956).

meaningful content and rational conclusions, but which is in fact often almost entirely devoid of their significance or sense. The non sequiturs of mass media advertising are notorious and unworthy of illustration. Partially as a reaction to this all-embracing atmosphere in modern life and partially in reinforcement of it, not a few media people (such as disk jockeys) have given up virtually all semblance of rational communication and now speak as rapidly, loudly, and nonsensically as possible, endeavoring to parallel in their discourse the rhythm, ear-shattering intensity, and total emotionality of the pop music they play. The more theoretically or philosophically inclined among them justify such use of the media on the ground that the future demands a new and revolutionary mode of communication, as little dependent on the past as the computer is on words or as the drug experience and the eastern mysticisms are on the verbal and rational structures of western thought.[37]

Arguments along this line, however, are wrongheaded at best and dangerous at worst. Computers do not somehow bypass ordinary thinking or rational communication; the entire computer concept, involving a binary language in which one must always choose "yes" or "no," is strictly founded on the law of noncontradiction.[38] As I have pointed out elsewhere, the computer will not even permit a neoorthodox dialectic of yes *and* no, to say nothing of the Bultmannian hermeneutical circle or a mystical transcending of the subject-object distinction.[39] The

---

[37]See John H. Garabedian and Orde Coombs, *Eastern Religions in the Electric Age* (New York: Grosset & Dunlap, 1969), *passim*.

[38]J.C.R. Licklider, *Libraries of the Future* (Cambridge, Mass: M.I.T. Press, 1965), pp. 126, 154–56, 191.

[39]Montgomery, *Computers, Cultural Change, and the Christ. Les ordinateurs, l'ordre culturel et le Christ. Komputer, kultureller Wandel und Christus* (Wayne, N.J. [now San Juan Capistrano, Calif.]: Christian Research Institute, 1969).

drug experience is a trip to *un*reality, not to greater meaningfulness: "French psychedelic specialist Roger Heim noted that under the influence of the drug (LSD) his handwriting, in reality black, appeared red; and a cat, given the drug, recoils in fear from a mouse."[40] As for the eastern mysticisms, like drugs, their openness to all possibilities and their refusal to communicate a specific content make them perilous in the extreme. Ponder Arthur Koestler's disillusioning judgment following a pilgrimage to the founts of eastern wisdom:

> At the start of this discussion of Zen, I quoted a few lines attributed to Seng-ts'an, who lived in the sixth century A.D., and was the Third Patriarch—that is, second in succession to the Bodhidharma. They are from his work *Hsin-hsin Ming*, which is regarded as the oldest Zen poem and one of its basic texts:
>
>> Be not concerned with right and wrong
>> The conflict between right and wrong
>> Is the sickness of the mind.

Fourteen centuries later, the last Patriarch (Suzuki) reaffirms the unbroken continuity of Zen's ethical relativism:

> "Zen is . . . extremely flexible in adapting itself to almost any philosophy and moral doctrine as long as its intuitive teaching is not interfered with. It may be found wedded to anarchism or fascism, communism or democracy, atheism or idealism."

The difference between the two statements is in their historical setting, and in their degrees of concreteness. The first comes from a Buddhist-Taoist mystic, who looks with a smiling shrug at the sententious pedantries of Confucian society. The second could come from a philosophically

---

[40]Montgomery, "The Gospel According to LSD," in his *Principalities and Powers*, p. 190.

minded Nazi journalist, or from one of the Zen monks who became suicide pilots.[41]

To be sure, it is this very ambiguity—this kaleidoscopic fluidity—that appeals to the modern media man. Impatient with the restraints of language, he delights in the nonlanguage of the koan:

Question: Everybody has a place of birth. Where is your place of birth?

Answer: Early this morning I ate white rice gruel. Now I'm hungry again.

Question: How is my hand like the Buddha's hand?

Answer: Playing the lute under the moon.

Question: How is my foot like a donkey's foot?

Answer: When the white heron stands in the snow it has a different colour.[42]

But our chameleonic media maniac (for thus he quickly becomes as he constantly changes color while eating white rice gruel) forgets two principles of the utmost importance for all communication: (1) Language cannot be transcended, for it is a defining mark of man *qua* man; and (2) Language is meaningful in direct proportion to its correspondence with reality.

First, no matter how sophisticated the technique of modern mass communication, there is no bypassing of language. Those who claim that language is nonessential to communication prove its essentiality by using it to present their claim. In this respect, language parallels

---

[41]Arthur Koestler, *The Lotus and the Robot* (New York: Macmillan, 1961), pp. 270–71.

[42]These 11th century koans, known as the "Three Barriers of Hung-Lun," are the oldest of which we have record; they are quoted from Alan W. Watts, *The Way of Zen* (London, 1957), p. 106.

logic: one must use it to argue against it, so opposition is futile per se. As Emerson said of Brahma, "When me they fly, I am the wings." The labors of one of the foremost linguistic theorists of our time has given this epistemological fact-of-life a solid ontological base. Noam Chomsky has collected overwhelming evidence in support of his contention that language is fundamental to the very nature of the human being, and qualitatively (not just quantitatively) sets man apart from all other creatures. He writes in summary:

Anyone concerned with the study of human nature and human capacities must somehow come to grips with the fact that all normal humans acquire language, whereas acquisition of even its barest rudiments is quite beyond the capacities of an otherwise intelligent ape—a fact that was emphasized, quite correctly, in Cartesian philosophy. It is widely thought that the extensive modern studies of animal communication challenge this classical view; and it is almost universally taken for granted that there exists a prob lem of explaining the "evolution" of human language from systems of animal communication. However, a careful look at recent studies of animal communication seems to me to provide little support for these assumptions. Rather, these studies simply bring out even more clearly the extent to which human language appears to be a unique phenomenon, without significant analogue in the animal world. If this is so, it is quite senseless to raise the problem of explaining the evolution of human language from more primitive systems of communication that appear at lower levels of intellectual capacity. . . .

As far as we know, possession of human language is associated with a specific type of mental organization, not simply a higher degree of intelligence. There seems to be no substance to the view that human language is simply a more complex instance of something to be found elsewhere in the animal world. This poses a problem for the biologist, since, if true, it is an example of true "emergence"—the appearance of a qualitatively different phenomenon at a specific stage of complexity of organization. Recognition of this fact, though formulated in entirely different terms, is what motivated much of the classical study of language by those whose primary concern was the nature of mind. And it seems to me that today there is no better or more promising way to explore the essential and distinctive properties of human intelligence than through the detailed investigation of the structure of this unique human possession.[43]

It is not therefore merely an epithet when the disk-jockey style of communication is regarded as "animal": here is indeed manifested a "more primitive system of communication that appears at lower levels of intellectual capacity." More significantly, one witnesses in such attempts at nonlanguage an abandonment of the uniquely human gift of genuine verbal behavior.

In the second place, the language which constitutes a defining mark of the human being is truly language to the precise extent that it mirrors reality. The analytical movement in philosophy, stemming from the work of the great Ludwig Wittgenstein, has brought this profound truth home to contemporary thought. Wittgenstein gave new life to the classic "correspondence theory" of truth (first presented formally by Plato and Aristotle) in the so-called "picture theory of language" set forth in his *Tractatus Logico-Philosophicus*: language by its very na-

---

[43]Noam Chomsky, *Language and Mind* (New York: Harcourt, Brace & World, 1968), pp. 59–62. As an example of his point, Chomsky cites the following case (p. 85): "Modern attempts to train apes in behavior that the investigator regards as language-like confirm this incapacity. . . . Ferster attempted to teach chimpanzees to match the binary numbers 001, . . ., 111 to sets of one to seven objects. He reports that hundreds of thousands of trials were required for 95 percent accuracy to be achieved, even in this trivial task. Of course, even at this stage the apes had not learned the principle of binary arithmetic." See also Chomsky's devastating review of behaviorist B.F. Skinner's *Verbal Behavior: Language*, Vol. 35, No. 1 (1959), pp. 26–58.

ture pictures or mirrors external reality.[44] In his later thinking, as reflected in the *Philosophische Untersuchungen (Philosophical Investigations)*, Wittgenstein, though turning his attention to noncognitive forms of discourse, never ceased to emphasize the fundamental principle that language must carry out its proper "work," that is, to mirror reality.[45] *Die Verwirrungen, die uns beschäftigen, entstehen gleichsam, wenn die Sprache leerläuft, nicht wenn sie arbeitet* (The confusions which occupy us arise when language is like an engine idling, not when it is doing work).[46] *Die philosophischen Probleme entstehen, wenn die Sprache feiert* (Philosophical problems arise when language *goes on holiday*).[47] The validity of this position can well be seen in the Austin-Strawson debate on the nature of truth, where J. L. Austin, though operating with a view of correspondence weaker than Wittgenstein's, is easily able to show that there is no meaningful alternative to "the rather boring yet satisfactory relation between words and world."[48]

But it is exactly this relation between words and world that is collapsing in so many areas of mass communication

---

[44]See, in the spite of its limitations, the invaluable essay on Wittgenstein's *Tractatus* by my former professor Max Black, which focuses on the "picture theory"; it appears in Black's *Language and Philosophy* (Ithaca, N.Y.: Cornell University Press, 1949), pp. 139–65, and serves as an excellent introduction to Black's later commentary, *A Companion to Wittgenstein's 'Tractatus'* (Ithaca, N.Y.: Cornell University Press, 1964).

[45]Cf. C.B. Daly, "New Light on Wittgenstein," *Philosophical Studies* (Maynooth, Ireland: St. Patrick's College), Vol. 10 (1960), pp. 5–49, especially pp. 46–49, where the unity of Wittgenstein's epistemological thought is well demonstrated.

[46]Ludwig Wittgenstein, *Philosophische Untersuchungen*. [*Philosophical Investigations*] 2nd ed. (Oxford: Blackwell, 1958), Pt. 1, para. 132. The English translator is G.E.M. Anscombe.

[47]*Ibid.*, para 38.

[48]J.L. Austin, in *Truth*, ed. George Pitcher ("Contemporary Perspectives in Philosophy"; Englewood Cliffs, N.J.: Prentice-Hall, 1964), p. 31.

today. Our disk jockey who emotes without saying anything is perhaps only the mildest example. The advertiser who hawks his product on the basis of false analogies and misleading rhetoric is a more serious phenomenon. The perverse propaganda of modern totalitarianism displays the full horror of separating language from reality and employing it, as in George Orwell's solipsistic cacotopia *1984*, to create a counter-world of demonic unreality, in which all values are inverted. C. S. Lewis, with his characteristic perception, sees these degenerations as the product of the modern, secular disengagement of language from referential reality:

As words become exclusively emotional they cease to be words and therefore of course cease to perform any strictly linguistic function. They operate as growls or barks or tears. "Exclusively" is an important adverb here. They die as words not because there is too much emotion in them but because there is too little—and finally nothing at all—of anything else. . . .

We have all heard *bolshevist*, *fascist*, *Jews*, and *capitalist*, used not to describe but merely to insult. Rose Macaulay noticed a tendency to prefix "so called" to almost any adjective when it was used of those the speaker hated; the final absurdity being reached when people referred to the Germans as "these so-called Germans." *Bourgeois* and *middle class* often suffer the same fate. . . .

This is the downward path which leads to the graveyard of murdered words. First they are purely descriptive; *adolescent* tells us a man's age, *villain*, his status. Then they are specifically pejorative; *adolescent* tells us that a man's work displays "mawkishness and all the thousand bitters" confessed by Keats, and *villain* tells that a man has a churl's mind and manners. Then they become *mere* pejoratives, useless synonyms for *bad*, as *villain* did and as *adolescent* may do if we aren't careful. Finally they become terms of abuse and cease to be language in the full sense at all.[49]

Yet how can the secular communicator prevent this devolution of language from taking place? Insofar as he remains secular—insofar as he separates himself from the Christian Logos—he *cannot,* for his language remains "on a holiday," disengaged from ultimate reality. As a self-centered, fallen man, he inevitably builds towers of Babel in a pitifully unrealistic endeavor to reach ultimacy by his own efforts, and the result is always what it was at Babel: the confusion of tongues. To put the linguistic mechanism back to work again one must become convinced of the essential relationship between language and reality, and then bring communication into accord with whatsoever things are true, honest, just, pure, lovely, and of good report (Phil. 4:8). But this will occur only when the communicator has acquired this perspective himself, and such a radical change in values necessitates the transformation of personality which only the eternal Word can effect.

In short, the secular communicator needs to be saved, and the only way he can encounter the saving Logos is through biblical proclamation. In contact with the Christ of Scripture, he can "with unveiled face reflect as a mirror the glory of the Lord and be transformed into the same image" (2 Cor. 3:18). Henry Drummond rightly termed this truth "the formula of sanctification,"[50] noting that men become like those they love and emulate. When Christ places the image of Himself in us by His Holy Spirit, we are changed into His likeness. The Triune God,

---

[49]C.S. Lewis, *Studies in Words* (Cambridge, Eng: Cambridge University Press, 1960), pp. 324–28.

[50]Henry Drummond, *The Changed Life* (Westwood, N.J.: Fleming H. Revell, n.d.).

who perfectly communicated Himself to us in the incarnate Logos, can indeed impart the respect for linguistic reality so desperately needed by the media of today. Mass communication needs scriptural proclamation in as fundamental a way as the church needs to recognize how God's plan for the ages is a cosmic communication.

THE TASK BEFORE US AND THE AVAILABLE DYNAMIC

And here the ball is thrown back to the Christian communicator: for it is he who has the responsibility and privilege of proclaiming the biblical message to the secular man of today. What an overwhelming task it appears to be! And, if we fail, how terrible the consequences—C. S. Lewis' graveyard of language and Orwell's *1984!*

As we review the conditions for communication, the responsibility seems even more crushing when we recall the necessity of making a message "appropriate to the group situation in which the receiver finds himself at the time when he is moved to make the desired response" (Schramm's fourth condition). How can we succeed in establishing such relevance in a world that, through the media, becomes more secular as every day goes by? Schramm underscores this point tellingly in his discussion of the low predictive effect of modern communication on personal value-systems:

> There are two things we can say with confidence about predicting communication effects. One is that a message is much more likely to succeed if it fits the patterns of understandings, attitudes, values, and goals that a receiver has; or, at least, if it starts with this pattern and tries to reshape it slightly. . . . It is very hard to change the minds of convinced Republicans or Democrats through communication, or even to get them to listen to the arguments of the opposing party. On the other hand, it is possible to start with a Republican or Democratic viewpoint and slightly

modify the existing party viewpoints in one way or another. . . .

The second thing we can say with confidence about communication effects is that they are resultants of a number of forces, of which the communicator can really control only one. The sender, that is, can shape his message and can decide when and where to introduce it. But the message is only one of at least four important elements that determine what response occurs. The other three are (a) the situation in which the communication is received and in which the response, if any, must occur; (b) the personality state of the receiver; and (c) his group relationships and standards. This is why it is so dangerous to try to predict exactly what will be the effect of any message except the simplest one in the simplest situation.

Let us take an example. In Korea, in the first year of the war there, I was interviewing a North Korean prisoner of war who had recently surrendered with one of our surrender leaflets on his person. It looked like an open and shut case: the man had picked up the leaflet, thought it over, and decided to surrender. But I was interviewing him anyway, trying to see just how the leaflet had its effect. This is what he told me.

He said that when he picked up the leaflet, it actually made him fight harder. It rather irritated him, and he didn't like the idea of having to surrender. He wasn't exactly a warlike man; he had been a clerk and was quiet and rather slow, but the message actually aroused a lot of aggression in him. Then the situation deteriorated. His division was hit hard and thrown back, and he lost contact with the command post. He had no food, except what he could find in the fields, and little ammunition. What was left of his company was isolated by itself in a rocky valley. Even then, he said, the morale was good, and there was no talk of surrendering. As a matter of fact, he said, the others would have shot him if he tried to surrender. But then a couple of our planes spotted them, shot up their hideout, and dropped some napalm. When it was over, he found himself alone, a half mile from where he had been, with half his jacket burned off, and no sign of any of his company. A couple of hours later some of our tanks came along. And only then did the leaflet have an effect. He remembered it had told him to surrender with his hands up, and he did so.

In other words, the communication had no effect (even had an opposite effect from the one intended) so long as the situation, the personality, and the group norms were not favorable.[51]

Like the disciples, our first tendency is to cry: "Who then can be saved?" If the best of modern persuasion by the media generally does not go beyond the "slight re-shaping" of existing patterns of belief and if the effect of the message is so often negated by the total situation which it enters, what can one expect for a message that is radically disharmonious with the fallen state of mankind and directly inimical to the sinner's fixation to save himself at all costs?

The answer—and it is fully sufficient—lies in the unique nature of the biblical proclamation. This is a message without equal. Of all the messages ever communicated, it is the only one so impregnated with the $\delta\dot{\nu}\nu\alpha\mu\iota\varsigma$ $\Theta\epsilon o\tilde{\nu}$ that it cannot return void (Isa. 55:11). Indeed, the message *is* this power of God, for it is the gospel (Rom. 1:16), the Word of the Cross (1 Cor. 1: 18), Christ Himself (1 Cor. 1: 24). This message is the only communication that can literally turn the receiver's world upside down (Acts 17:6). The dynamic of the gospel message is such that by its very nature it produces saving faith, for "faith cometh by hearing, and hearing $\delta\iota\grave{\alpha}$ $\dot{\rho}\dot{\eta}\mu\alpha\tau o\varsigma$ $\chi\rho\iota\sigma\tauo\tilde{\nu}$" (Rom. 10:17). The power of the biblical proclamation offers no opportunity for Christian irresponsibility or indifference to the best techniques of communicating it relevantly vis-à-vis the sinner's situation, but at the same time it offers an absolute deterrent to despair in the face of seem-ingly overwhelming secular odds.

---

[51]Schramm, "Procedures and Effects of Mass Communication," pp. 124–27.

Another way of viewing this same magnificent truth is provided by the mass communicator's "fraction of selection":

$$\frac{\text{Expectation of Reward}}{\text{Effort Required}}$$

Schramm notes that mass communications entail a particularly frustrating unpredictability of effect as compared with ordinary communication, for feedback occurs so seldom and in a partial and inadequate way (how many radio listeners write to the announcers or the sponsors?). Faced with the necessity of "flying blind," the mass communicator needs to rely on the fraction of selection. He will succeed if he recognizes that "you can increase the value of that fraction either by increasing the numerator or decreasing the denominator, which is to say that an individual is more likely to select a certain communication if it promises him more reward or requires less effort than comparable communications."[52]

Here again we see the uniqueness of the biblical message of salvation, and perhaps gain some insight into why it cannot return void. Presented in its fullness—without the adulteration of rationalistic criticism or the confusion of law and gospel—the biblical proclamation is the only message on earth whose fraction of selection is literally

$$\frac{100\%}{0}$$

This is the case because Scripture promises the sinner, as expectation, no less than reconciliation with the God of

[52]*Ibid.*, p. 129.

the universe, both in time and eternity; and it demands (praise God) no human effort whatsoever: "For by grace are ye saved through faith; and that not of yourselves: it is the gift of God" (Eph. 2:8). The effort was God's—even to the giving of His own Son—and the wondrous expectation of life and peace is ours, through His love.

As Christian communicators then, we can take heart. "Greater is he that is in you, than he that is in the world" (1 John 4:4). If we see that the biblical proclamation, by its very nature, requires to be communicated, and recognize that the only hope for the world of mass communication is Jesus Christ, then God will Himself win the battle for us. Martin Luther, who of all the towering saints in the history of the church perhaps best wedded an unadulterated biblical proclamation with the best mass communication his epoch afforded, tells us precisely where our confidence should lie:

> *Mit unser macht ist nichts gethan,*
> *wir sind gar bald verloren:*
> *Es streit fur uns der rechte man,*
> *den Gott hat selbs erkoren.*
> *Fragstu, wer der ist?*
> *er heist Jhesu Christ,*
> *der Herr Zebaoth,*
> *und ist kein ander Gott,*
> *das felt mus er behalten.*[53]

---

[53]Stanza 2 of the earliest High German text now accessible of Luther's *Ein' feste Burg ist unser Gott* (A Mightly Fortress Is Our God): *Geisliche Lieder* (Wittenberg, 1531), transcribed in C.E.Ph. Wackernagel, *Das deutsche Kirchenlied* (5 vols., Leipzig, 1864–1877), Vol. 3, pp. 19–21, E.T. by Thomas Carlyle:

> With force of arms we nothing can,
>   Full soon were we down-ridden,
> But for us fights the proper Man
>   Whom God Himself hath bidden.
>   Ask ye who is this same?
>   Christ Jesus is His name,
>   The Lord Sabaoth's Son;
>   He, and no other one,
> Shall conquer in the battle.

10
The Fuzzification of Biblical Inerrancy

Harold Lindsell's *Battle for the Bible* has been widely castigated for troubling Zion. Writing in a special issue of the Fuller Theological Seminary Alumni magazine, *Theology, News, and Notes,* Clark Pinnock expostulates, ''What a pity to see the admirable unity of the evangelical caucus now being threatened just as it is beginning to bear fruit, and what irony that the editor of *Christianity Today,* the organ which was founded to facilitate evangelical harmony and cooperation and which more than anything else has symbolized that unity, should be the person responsible for placing it in jeopardy.''

But Pinnock gives the editor of *Christianity Today* too much credit (or discredit). The internal conflict in evangelicalism over the extent of biblical reliability has been simmering for decades; all *The Battle for the Bible* did was to make journalistically explicit what has for long been recognized implicitly. Hardly had I settled into my professorial chair at the Trinity Evangelical Divinity

School in 1963, than I got to know theologically astute
Inter-Varsity staff worker Tom Stark (now a campus
pastor at Michigan State University at East Lansing).
Tom had become so disturbed by the rumors of a shift
from unqualified belief in the inerrant Scripture at Fuller
Seminary that, disbelieving these rumors and wanting to
lay the ghost to rest firsthand, he spent a week there at his
own expense, interviewing students and faculty, sitting in
on classes, etc. On his return he told me that he "had sent
his last Inter-Varsity student there."

From June 20 to 29, 1966, I agonized through the
"Wenham Conference"—the Seminar on the Authority
of Scripture held at Gordon College under the chairman-
ship of Harold John Ockenga. The *raison d'être* of this
conference was to arrive at a united evangelical front on
biblical authority, but the participants, well representing
the world evangelical scene, were deeply and hopelessly
divided on the inerrancy issue. Indeed, the papers presented at the conference were never published for that
very reason. I will always remember the conversational
marathon between John Gerstner and Daniel Fuller.
Gerstner, like Socrates trying to draw geometry maieuti-
cally out of a slave boy in the *Meno,* endeavored by
careful and compelling questions to get Fuller to see the
need unqualifiedly to affirm Scripture's inerrancy; to the
bitter end, at each crucial juncture in the argument, Fuller
would reply (see Mark 4:31), "But the mustard seed *isn't*
the smallest of all seeds!" Sad to say, Pinnock's "admirable unity of the evangelical caucus," relative to the extent
of biblical reliability, is more a myth than a reality,
and—whatever else may be said for or against *The Battle
for the Bible*—it has to be seen as an honest piece of
demythologizing.

FUZZIFICATION AND HERMENEUTICS

The foregoing historical vignette might well give the impression that the "battle for the Bible" is a clean-cut war between those evangelicals who affirm the Bible's inerrancy and those who do not. At the Wenham Conference—under controlled, private conditions—this was largely the case. But it is certainly not true of the current Bible battle being waged in the public arena, where denominational and seminary loyalties are at stake and where the continuing existence of evangelical institutions depends squarely on the confidence of lay contributors (both the millionaire and the little old lady in tennis shoes).

Here one of the processes so admirably described by Washington's Dr. James H. Boren, founder of INATA-PROBU (the International Association of Professional Bureaucrats) enters the picture: *fuzzification*. "Fuzzification," defined by Boren as "the presentation of a matter in terms that permit adjustive interpretation," (see *Time*, November 29, 1976, p. 13) occurs especially, though not exclusively, where organizational or other social pressure dictates "adjustment." And adjustment is achieved through "interpretation"—in theological parlance, hermeneutics.

Specifically, if the loss of the term "inerrancy" (or "Infallibility" or other powerful language affirming biblical authority) is fraught with sufficiently dire consequences, there will be the strongest temptation to retain these expressions while giving the Bible such "adjustive interpretation" that negatively critical approaches to it can be employed anyway. Well before evangelicals began to carry out such operations, Roman Catholic and Lutheran theologians—whose learning and sophistication put today's evangelical fuzzifiers to shame—were already engaged in the task of having their cake (retaining "inerrancy") and eating it too (treating Scripture critically). Brief examples will help us to appreciate the parallel phenomenon in the evangelicalism of the present moment.

The Roman Catholic As Hermeneutic Fuzzifier

At the Council of Trent the Roman Church declared that it believed the sacred Scriptures to be infallibly true—indeed "dictated either orally by Christ or by the Holy Ghost" (4th Session, 8 April 1546; Denzinger, 783). On this basis, Pius IX (1846–1878) condemned those who held that "prophecies and miracles in the Sacred Text are poetical commentary" or that the Bible contains "mythical constructions" (Denzinger, 1707); Pius X (1903–1914) dealt similarly with the modernists, expressly rejecting partial inspiration theories, higher critical documentary theories, and all "dismembering of the [Scriptural] records" (Denzinger, 2011, 2100, 2102).

With the excommunication of outspoken modernists such as Loisy, discretion became the better part of valor. As George Lindbeck of Yale has noted, modernism simply went underground in the Roman Church, to surface again in a different guise a generation or so later. The new guise? While affirming biblical inerrancy, one takes the very same positions the modernists did relative to scriptural errors, contradictions, source theories, and the like but explains and justifies this seemingly inconsistent approach as a question of *hermeneutics*, not of inspiration at all! I have cited numerous examples in my essay, "The Approach of New Shape Roman Catholicism to Scriptural Inerrancy" (in my *Ecumenicity, Evangelicals, and Rome* and also in *The Inerrant Word of God*). Of Myles Bourke's elimination of many historical details in Matthew 1–2 on the ground that the infancy narratives should be interpreted as a haggadic, midrash commentary, James M. Robinson has approvingly noted: "Form criticism has made it possible for the Catholic scholar to assert that the literal sense of a given passage is not to present a true story but rather a story conveying truth."

Similarly, on the question of the pope's infallibility, The Vatican Council of 1870 declared that when the pope speaks *ex cathedra,* defining a doctrine of faith or morals for the whole Church, he speaks infallibly. (Denzinger, 1839). When Hans Küng expressly rejected this teaching in his book *Infallible? An Inquiry* (English trans., 1971), other Roman Catholic scholars, though in substantial agreement with Küng's views, were mindful of the strategic importance of retaining the terminology of Vatican I. Solution? Simply interpret "infallibility" so as to have your cake and eat it too. Thus Gregory Baum, writing in *The Infallibility Debate* (ed. John J. Kirvan, 1971), performs the needed hermeneutic fuzzification:

> While we separate ourselves from the literal meaning of Vatican I, we preserve and affirm its essential Christian witness. Thanks to this special gift of truth, the Church is able to take her own religious experience seriously, discern the center of the Gospel in her age, and reinterpret her dogma in its light as a message that continues to address people, that makes sense to them, and that initiates them into a new consciousness.

Lutheran Fuzzification

Among Protestants, Lutherans are perhaps most like Roman Catholics in their concern for explicit and comprehensive doctrinal formulations. In contrast to most Protestants, Lutherans—in the expression of the late professor Dr. Hermann Sasse—know how to "think theologically." Understandably then, when Lutheran theologians have desired to take the modern critical approach to the Bible, they have been unable simply to dump the idea of scriptural inerrancy. The *Formula of Concord,* to which Lutheran pastors subscribe confessionally, asserts, "Luther explicitly made this distinction between divine and human writings: God's Word alone is and should remain the only standard and norm of all teachings, and no human being's writings dare be put on a par with it, but everything must be subjected to it."[10]

The modern Lutheran theologian is thus compelled to fuzzify: the term "inerrancy" is retained, but it is hermeneutically redefined to allow for the full range of negative biblical criticism. Typical of this approach is the pamphlet by John D. Frey, *Is the Bible Inerrant?,* widely distributed by the break-away "Seminex" group that is in process of separating from the Lutheran Church-Missouri Synod. "How is it possible for the Bible to be inerrant if it contains faulty science, inaccurate quotations, and various discrepancies?" asks Frey, with the insouciance of the one who first posed the parallel question, "Have you stopped beating your wife?" Frey's answer: "It is possible because inerrancy does not mean an absence of all inaccuracies and discrepancies, but that the Bible says what it intends to say and what it intends to say corresponds to fact. Inerrancy is determined by intended teaching, and not by the concepts of science or details of history used to convey that teaching."

A New Evangelical Hermeneutic

The preceding Roman Catholic and Lutheran examples should prepare us for the most recent bend in the river of evangelical thinking on the inerrancy issue. Rather than reject the word "inerrancy," why not simply define it so that it no longer poses any threat to biblical interpretation? The Spring, 1976, issue of the *Evangelical Theological Society Journal,* under the editorship of Ronald Youngblood of the Bethel Theological Seminary, offers many examples of this trend. We shall restrict ourselves to the lead article by Grant R. Osborne: "Redaction Criticism and the Great Commission: A Case Study toward a Biblical Understanding of Inerrancy."

Osborne argues in reference to the Trinitarian formula in Matthew 28:19 that Jesus apparently did not utter it (even though it is preceded by the words, "Jesus came and spoke to them, saying"): 'it seems most likely that at some point the tradition or Matthew expanded an original monadic formula." Such redaction criticism, he assures us, poses no threat to an evangelical understanding of biblical inerrancy; rather, it is "a tremendous, positive tool for understanding the early Church and its theology." The redaction of Jesus' words by the biblical writers and the early church creates no problem, for the redaction was Spirit-led and inerrant! The mere fact that "it is difficult, if not impossible, to trace the exact words that Jesus spoke on the mountain in Galilee" ought not to worry us; after all, "the evangelists did not attempt to give us *ipsissima verba* but rather sought to interpret Jesus' words for their audiences. In other words, they wished to make Jesus' teachings meaningful to their own *Sitz im Leben* rather than to present them unedited. Relevancy triumphed over verbal exactness." Thus can "verbal inexactitude" be harmonized hermeneutically with the Evangelical Theological Society's doctrinal statement, "The Bible alone, and the Bible in its entirety, is the Word of God written, and is therefore inerrant in the autographs."

REDUCTIO AD FUZZIFACTUM

Some years ago, in the throes of the Lutheran controversy over biblical authority, I wrote:

Whenever we reach the point of affirming on the one hand that the Bible is infallible or inerrant and admitting on the other hand to internal contradictions of factual inaccuracies within it, we not only make a farce of language, promoting ambiguity, confusion, and perhaps even deception in the church; more reprehensible than even these things, we in fact deny the plenary inspiration and authority of Scripture, regardless of the theological formulae we may insist on retaining.

A way-out illustration will show why this critique is no exaggeration.

Suppose I were to declare that Lincoln's Gettysburg Address is inerrant. You might very well try to point out errors in it to disabuse me of my patriotic but loonish new religion. You might say, for example, that the "new nation" was not brought forth on this continent exactly eighty-seven years earlier, or that, as a matter of fact, the world *has* "noted and long remembered what we say here." But to each such objection I counter that the author's intent was never to say that *anyway:* "inerrancy is determined by intended teaching, and not by details used to convey that teaching." Any fault you find with the Address, I class as a "detail," and so the inerrancy of the document is never touched by it. Or suppose that when you say that you don't believe Lincoln ever spoke those very words, I reply that I don't either, but they are still inerrantly his because those who recorded them infallibly interpreted them in accord with Lincoln's intent, making them maximally relevant to their "life situation."

You could not help but conclude that I was beyond hope—for such a doctrine of inerrancy, being compatible with any and every contrary piece of evidence, is technically meaningless. Nothing can count against it. Such a claim could be made for *any* book as readily as it could for the Gettysburg Address (or the Bible). Errors are always "adjustively interpreted"—fuzzified—so they can be accepted as mere unintended "details" or the results of

Spirit-inspired redaction. The "inerrancy" with which one is left is an inerrancy devoid of meaningful content.

HOW TO DEFUZZIFY BIBLICAL INERRANCY

The doctrine of biblical inerrancy derives from the attitude of Scripture toward itself, and in particular the attitude of Christ toward Scripture. What we must recognize is that Scripture and its Christ do not give us an open concept of inspiration which we can fill in as the extra-biblical methodologies of our time appear to dictate. To the contrary, the total trust Jesus and the apostles displayed toward Scripture entails a precise and controlled hermeneutic. They subordinated the opinions and traditions of their day to Scripture; so must we. They did not regard Scripture as erroneous or self-contradictory; neither can we. They took its miracles and prophecies as literal fact; so must we. They regarded Scripture not as the product of editors and redactors but as stemming from Moses, David, and other immediately inspired writers; we must follow their lead. They believed that the events recorded in the Bible happened as real history; we can do no less.

With characteristic theological perception, the Commission on Theology and Church Relations of the Lutheran Church-Missouri Synod has prepared *A Statement of Scriptural and Confessional Principles* (available in a study edition from Box 201, St. Louis, Mo. 63166) to deal with the inerrancy controversy in Lutheranism. In line with historic Lutheran practice, this document not only sets forth positive affirmations ("theses") on biblical inerrancy; it simultaneously declares what will not be tolerated hermeneutically ("antitheses")—thereby preserving the doctrine of biblical authority from "adjustive interpretation." Thus after asserting affirmatively that "with Luther, we confess that 'God's Word cannot err,' " (LC,

IV, 57) the statement goes on to "reject the following views":

That the Scriptures are only functionally inerrant, that is, that the Scriptures are "inerrant" only in the sense that they accomplish their aim of bringing the Gospel of salvation to men.

That the Biblical authors accommodated themselves to using and repeating as true the erroneous notions of their day (for example, the claim that Paul's statements on the role of women in the church are not binding today because they are the culturally conditioned result of the apostle's sharing the views of contemporary Judaism as a child of his time).

That statements of Jesus and the New Testament writers concerning the human authorship of portions of the Old Testament or the historicity of certain Old Testament persons and events need not be regarded as true (for example, the Davidic authorship of Psalm 110, the historicity of· Jonah, or the fall of Adam and Eve). . . .

That Jesus did not make some of the statements or perform some of the deeds attributed to him in the Gospels but that they were in fact invented or created by the early Christian community or the evangelists to meet their specific needs.

That the Biblical authors sometimes placed statements into the mouths of people who in fact did not make them (for example, the claim that the "Deuteronomist" places a speech in Solomon's mouth which Solomon never actually made), or that they relate events as having actually taken place that did not in fact occur (for example, the fall of Adam and Eve, the crossing of the Red Sea on dry land, the episode of the brazen serpent, Jesus' cursing of the fig tree, John the Baptist's experiences in the wilderness, Jesus' changing water into wine, Jesus' walking on water, or even Jesus' bodily resurrection from the dead or the fact of His empty tomb).

That the use of certain "literary forms" necessarily calls into question the historicity of that which is being described (for example, that the alleged midrashic form of the infancy narratives in Matthew and Luke suggests that no virgin birth actually occurred, or that the literary form of Genesis 3 argues against the historicity of the Fall).

Recognizing that positive creedal affirmations of biblical reliability are no longer sufficient to preserve churches or institutions from the hermeneutic destruction of their bibliology, the Melodyland School of Theology in December, 1976, became the first theological seminary in the world to adopt a doctrinal statement with built-in hermeneutic commitments, designed to prevent the biblical paragraph of its credo from being evacuated of meaning by unscriptural interpretative methodology. Melodyland's doctrinal statement does not rest with its declaration that "the Scriptures in all that they affirm are without error, in the whole and in the part, and therefore are completely trustworthy"; it goes on to deal with the specific hermeneutic implications of belief in biblical inerrancy:

All genuine Christian Statements of Doctrine depend upon a proper interpretation of the Holy Scriptures. The Melodyland School of Theology, therefore, unreservedly commits itself to the following hermeneutic rules:

I. A passage of Holy Scripture is to be taken as true in its natural, literal sense unless the context of the passage itself indicates otherwise, or unless an article of faith established elsewhere in Scripture requires a broader understanding of the text.

II. The prime article of faith applicable to biblical interpretation is the attitude of Christ and His Apostles toward the Scriptures. Their utter trust in Scripture—in all it teaches—must govern the interpreter's practice, thus eliminating in principle any interpretation which sees the biblical texts as erroneous or self-contradictory.

III. Extra-biblical linguistic and cultural considerations must never decide the interpretation of a text; and any use of extra-biblical material to arrive at an interpretation inconsistent with the truth of a scriptural passage is to be rejected. Extra-biblical data can and should put critical questions to a text, but only Scripture itself can legitimately answer questions about itself.

IV. Not all literary forms are consistent with scriptural revelation. The interpreter must not appeal to destructive literary forms (such as mythology) which cast doubt on the reliability or the morality of the Divine Author of Scripture.

V. The interpreter should employ all tools of scholarly research that do not make experience, reason, or feeling the basis of interpretation. Such practices are identified by their assumptions, which either (as in demythologizing) do violence to articles of faith, or (like certain documentary theories) oppose the clarity of the authentic biblical texts and the factuality of the events recorded in them, or (like the so-called "new hermeneutic") give to the sinful cultural context, past and present, a definitive role in the formulation of biblical teaching. These and other unscriptural techniques are to be studiously avoided in carrying out the task of interpretation.

VI. Harmonization of apparent scriptural difficulties should be pursued within reasonable limits, and when harmonization would pass beyond such bounds, the interpreter must leave the problem open rather than, by assuming error, impugn the absolute truthfulness of God, who inspires all Holy Scripture for our salvation and learning. We hold with St. Augustine (*De Potent.*, IV, 1, 8): "If you chance upon anything [in Scripture] that does not seem to be true, you must not conclude that the sacred writer made a mistake; rather your attitude should be: the manuscript is faulty, or the version is not accurate, or you yourself do not understand the matter."

The defuzzing of biblical inerrancy requires nothing less than antitheses of the kind formulated by the Missouri Synod's Commission on Theology, and hermeneutic affirmations of the sort that Melodyland has made mandatory for its board of directors and faculty. The survival among us of the classic evangelical view of Scripture depends squarely on our recognition that the Bible must not become the victim of "adjustive interpretation."

THE SPECTRE OF EVANGELICAL DIVISION

We are warned that to press a consistent view of biblical inerrancy may divide evangelicalism. This was precisely Melanchthon's argument at the Diet of Augsburg in 1530 relative to the presentation of the Augsburg Confession to Charles V by the believing Protestant princes: "You may divide the Holy Roman Empire—you may even destroy it." Replied the electors: "We shall nonetheless confess our Christ."

The question, of course, is simply whether entire scriptural reliability is all that important. I believe it is. I would not tolerate for a moment the argument that because the Trinity is nowhere set forth by name in the Bible, evangelicalism must not be divided over that doctrine. Biblical inerrancy, though the expression does not appear in Scripture, is nevertheless Christ's view; and He must be my Lord in this as in all other areas. If He is not Lord of all, He is not Lord at all.

The Lutheran Church-Missouri Synod agonized over the loss of some professors, students, and congregations on this very issue, but she has rightly concluded that if unity must be preserved at the cost of *sola Scriptura*—of the formal principle of all theology—then the price of unity is far too high. The great theologies of Christendom have never been *via media* theologies, for Scripture and its Christ spew the lukewarm out of the mouth.

I frequently recall the Scottish revival in which the neighboring dominie asked: "And how many souls were added to the kirk?" "None," came the reply, "but we've gotten rid of a few we've been tryin' to get rid o' for years." *That* can also be a revival. Make no mistake. God will not let falter those who are consistently faithful to His Word. Whatever else may occur in Christendom, the ministry of childlike Bible believers will increase geometrically, for faith comes by hearing and hearing by the Word of God, and only the Word of God remains forever.

Appendix

Review of *Testing Christianity's Truth Claims: Approaches to Christian Apologetics,* by Gordon Lewis (Moody, 1976, 347 pp.).

This work is intended by its author, who is professor of systematic theology and Christian philosophy at the Conservative Baptist Seminary, Denver, to serve primarily as a college, Bible school, or seminary textbook in apologetics. Its readers are not expected to be philosophy majors and the book ends with a brief glossary of philosophical terms.

Lewis offers to the student descriptions and critiques of six "distinctive systems in defense of Christian truth claims," all the product of "orthodox and evangelical" thinkers who have "produced their major works since 1945": J. Oliver Buswell, Jr. (pure empiricism), Stuart Hackett (rational empiricism), Cornelius Van Til (biblical authoritarianism), Gordon Clark (rationalism), Earl E. Barrett (mysticism), and Edward John Carnell—to whose verificational approach to facts, the author devotes almost as much space (108 pages) as he does to the other five thinkers combined (130 pages).

An appendix of only forty-three pages treats the work of ten "recent writers on the issues that have been focal points through the book." They are, in the author's order of presentation: Francis Schaeffer, Os Guinness, Clark Pinnock, John Warwick Montgomery, Norman Geisler, George Mavrodes, Arthus Holmes, Josh McDowell, Bernard Ramm, and C. S. Lewis. Some of these appended thinkers, whose works are treated in an average of four pages each, are referred to as well in the annotated bibliographies to the major chapters, which consist of a potpourri of references to the thinkers' writings and a selection of other works that Lewis apparently considers either to parallel their viewpoints or to help in clarifying and interpreting them. There is no name or subject index to the volume.

Professor Lewis has an attractive personality, and I have had an excellent relationship with him; his contribution to the Christian Medical Society's recent symposium volume on *Demon Possession,* which I edited, was most helpful. I say this because I should like readers of this review to understand that it is painful for me to have to say that *Testing Christianity's Truth Claims* almost totally fails as an apologetic text or survey of the field. It can be recommended only as a reference work for libraries or for specialists who must consult all treatments of the subject. The problems of the book are so numerous that little more than a focus upon the two major areas of difficulty can be provided here.

Most serious is the overall imbalance of the work. Presumably the author intends to give student readers a general picture of current influential defenses of the Christian faith. From the space devoted to particular thinkers in Lewis's book, it would simply be impossible to acquire such a picture. Indeed, a bizarre portrait emerges. C. S. Lewis, unquestionably the most influential orthodox Christian apologist after World War II, is relegated to eight pages of appendix, with no mention whatever of the deep-myth side of his apologetic as developed conjointly with Charles Williams and J.R.R. Tolkien and as set forth in his science-fiction trilogy and Narnia chronicles. A full major chapter is devoted to Stuart Hackett, whose only book, *Resurrection of Theism,* has been out of print for years. (It was to have been followed by two volumes that unfortunately have not yet been published). Another major chapter is on Earl Barrett, whom I, after a decade of doing and teaching apologetics with more than average bibliographical interests, had not even heard of. The omission of semi-evangelical Peter Berger's remarkable sociological defense of the faith in his *Rumor of Angels* may be explained on the ground of Lewis's recurrent over-identification of apologetics with *philosophical* defenses; but what can possibly justify the general omission of the entire area of analytical apologetics (deriving from Wittgensteinian analytical philosophy) that has revolutionized so much contemporary defense of the faith? One thinks immediately of the work of Ian Ramsey, who gets only a single bibliographical citation, and of Jerry Gill and Alvin Plantinga, who receive none.

Secondly, there was a lack of comprehensive research and careful treatment of the thinkers presented. These failings are particularly evident in the appendix. Schaeffer's methodology is inadequately critiqued: no attempt is made to determine the key matter of how and why he chooses particular cultural illustrations for his "cultural apologetic." My position is superficially treated on the basis of my publications only up to 1969 (and none of the secondary journal articles or the theses devoted to my apologetic are used in the analysis at all). Geisler's position is described without any apparent awareness that it derives from and thoroughly reflects his commitment to an evangelically modified Thomism. Mavrodes is treated as if he were a mainline evangelical thinker, whereas he has expressly disengaged himself from the classical evangelical position on total biblical reliability (Lewis surely should have been aware of his American Scientific Affiliation [ASA] Journal articles on the subject). The muddiness of Arthur Holmes's efforts to have a variety of epistemological cakes and eat them too is only dimly perceived.

But not only in the appendix are such difficulties rife. Neither in his chapter on Buswell nor in his chapter on Van Til does Lewis cite or analyze the polemical articles these men wrote against each other—articles essential for the illumination of the apologetic issues between them. No effort is made to distinguish Dooyeweerd's position from Van Til's or to give even a brief description of the former's views, which are certainly as worthy of analysis as Van Til's and are in many ways far broader in application and influence. It is simply misleading for Lewis to say nothing more of Dooyeweerd's world-view than that it is "similar to that of Van Til" and then to quote Van Til: "I rejoice in the work of Christian philosophers like . . . Dooyeweerd."

Even Carnell, to whom four chapters are devoted, is not given the keen critique that his work deserves and that he almost invariably gave to others. His views are clearly set forth, but of the six major thinkers Lewis discusses it was Carnell who expressed himself the most clearly and therefore was in least need of exposition! (One thinks of the charwoman who found the Gospel of John a great help in understanding the commentary on it her bishop gave her).

Lewis never seems to see the fundamental problem with the "systematic consistency" truth-test Carnell took wholesale from his Boston University philosophy mentor, E. S. Brightman: what happens if internal consistency is incompatible with the fitting of the facts? That this is by no means a theoretical issue should be evident when we reflect upon such high matters of Christian doctrine as predestination and free will or the Most Holy Trinity. Christian doctrine isn't "internally consistent" at all points—at least not from a human perspective (and apologetics always speaks to fallen man in the human perspective, there being, presumably, no need for the discipline in heaven, where God's thoughts reign). Carnell never seemed to realize that if your truth-test is multiple, you must have a higher truth-test to arbitrate when the different aspects of the multiple test run into conflict. In the final analysis, one cannot stop with Carnell: either one must move to the fitting of the facts as the ultimate test of a world-view (in C. S. Lewis fashion) or one must decide that life isn't bigger than logic and conclude that what is consistent is therefore true. However, the greatest of the world's madmen have held the most consistent delusions—in contrast, note well, to the apostolic testimony: "We have not followed cunningly devised fables, when we made known unto you the power and coming of our Lord Jesus Christ, but were eyewitnesses of his majesty" (2 Pet. 1:16).

Name Index

235

Subject Index